SUN AND SHADOW

SUN AND SHADOW

Rose Resnick

New York

ATHENEUM

1975

Copyright © 1975 by Rose Resnick
All rights reserved
Library of Congress catalog card number 74-32614
ISBN 0-689-106-661
Published simultaneously in Canada by McClelland and Stewart Ltd.
Manufactured in the United States of America by
H. Wolff, New York
Designed by Kathleen Carey
First Edition

Preface

THOSE OF US who were children in the twenties were lucky in many ways. No one ever mentioned poverty then. If you happened to be poor, you knew you had a lot of company and nobody but you was going to do anything about it. Certainly not the government. The best thing the government did something about was education. Education was compulsory. If anyone was absent from school more than three days, a truant officer came around to talk to the parents, and pretty soon the truant was back in the fold again.

No one ever heard much about crime either. Oh, there was plenty of it around, but rarely did it affect the children in the street. Cops were friends who took lost kids home and directed traffic with a wave of the hand and a whistle.

I consider that I was lucky to have been poor, and to have had to fight my way out of it, lucky to have attended public schools with all shapes, types, and races of children, and lucky to have felt safe playing with them on the sidewalks of New York.

PREFACE

And there were other ways in which I was privileged —privileged to have had a mother as a model of work and sacrifice, to have had music in my bones, and to have known the influence of people with love, ideals, and a zest for living, the good contagions of the world. Through those gifts from the gods came twin careers— music and social work—and in them, a full, often joyous life.

I have also tried to show how a blind child acquires her impressions of the objective world, and how attitudes, rather than the lack of sight, are the real agony of blindness. As with all minorities, the deepest desire of those who cannot see is for equal opportunity and to be treated as human beings, capable of participating with their fellow men in recreation, education and employment, rather than as "blind" people. From agencies, they want only a voice in the policies that shape their destinies, the tools of independence, then to be set free.

If my story helps in even a small way to achieve these goals, it will have fulfilled its purposes.

ROSE RESNICK

Contents

1: My Family — 3
2: Just One of Her Eight — 14
3: Gateway to a Seeing World — 22
4: Mossyledge — 39
5: Transition — 46
6: My New Music Teacher — 57
7: Fontainebleau — 69
8: Début — 80
9: Solo in California — 90
10: Close-up of a Social Agency — 97
11: New Eyes in Morristown — 111
12: The Search Begins — 124
13: From Bach to Boogie — 135
14: Interlude at Yosemite — 151
15: On Tour — 162
16: A New Direction — 171
17: How Do You Build an Organization? — 181
18: Where the Trees Sing — 197
19: An Unfinished Opera — 221
20: A Fatal Decision — 237
21: Joy in the Morning — 262

SUN AND SHADOW

[1]

My Family

THEY CAME with the hordes that had fled the Russian pogroms at the turn of the century. It was September 1901. The flags were at half mast after McKinley's assassination. Leah and Harris Resnick, with the first four of their children—Fanny, Nathan, David, Ida—settled in a five-room flat on Manhattan's Lower East Side. Here, a little over a year apart, Sarah, Jean, Becky, and I were born.

On the doorpost of the railroad flat hung the mezuzah, a rolled-up parchment inscribed with passages from the Bible, believed to bring good luck. Just inside the door, between the kitchen and dining room, was space for the dumbwaiter which brought ice up from the basement and garbage down. The kitchen, to the right of the door, was just big enough for a sink, an icebox, a washtub (which doubled as a bathtub), and a black iron coal-stove which Mother polished until, as the neighbors said, you could see yourself in it. In the dining room, a huge, round, oilcloth-covered table stood between two narrow double-hung windows that looked out on the next tenement. Against the opposite wall of the room, a china closet housed cut-glass bowls (heaven knows where they came from) and the special set of dishes used at Passover.

Next came two tiny bedrooms. Jean and I shared the bed and dresser in the first; Sarah and Becky doubled up in the other. The "front room," facing the street, was my parents' bedroom.

They had grown up on a farm in the Russian Ukraine. I remember hearing Mama talk about washing clothes in the nearby river, spading the earth, cutting hay, shoveling coal, making all their own bread. But here in the new land, close to New York's burgeoning apparel-center, and like so many other Russian immigrants at the time, Papa took up tailoring. Little wonder that, although he had a sharp eye for line and learned the trade quickly, tailoring bored him and took one tenth of his energies.

He was a big man, handsome, imposing; almost six feet, broad-chested, erect. He had a thick neck, jutting chin and regular features. His hair was close-cropped. When he entered a room, he dominated it. His natural tone of voice was firm and loud. He treated his family as though he were a commandant rather than a father.

When he got angry, which was very often, he shouted at us. Sometimes he even threw things. One night he hurled a bowl of cube sugar at Ida. We all flew from the table in terror. Mother remained silent. After such tirades, we tried to persuade Mother to leave him, but her Old World notions, her stoicism, her ignorance of how to proceed, and her concern for feeding the family made this impossible.

Besides, she was just plain afraid of the man. It was understandable—he was twice her size and she hated confrontations. She knew that if she uttered a word in self-defense it would only touch off yet bigger explosions. Meek, docile, she put up with his violence, his demands, his complaints while he was around. Then, when he was gone, she would moan to us about her fate.

"What did I do to deserve him? He's never satisfied. If only God will let me have a few years to live in peace after he goes."

But Papa had a completely different side. In his better moods he could entertain us with roguish accounts of his day's experiences.

At the supper table one night he had us giggling at the bad time he had given an optician.

"Today I went to have my eyes examined," he said. "Instead he's turning me around and around, looking in my ears.

" 'Doctor,' I said, 'you're an eyeglass doctor. You won't charge me for looking in my ears, will you?'

" 'I'm not looking in your ears, my dear man.'

"I said, 'You're turning me from side to side—I'm getting dizzy.'

" 'Well,' he said, 'I have to measure the size of your head for the frames.'

" 'But frames I don't need,' I told him. 'I can use the old ones.'

"Then he starts covering up one eye. I said, 'Doctor, how can you test my eyes if you're covering one up?'

" 'My dear man, we must test each eye separately.'

"'But doctor,' I told him, 'I never use one eye at a time. I use them both together. Doctor, if you give me glasses for one eye, we'll change places. I'll send you the bill.'"

He loved to reminisce about his pranks on the inspectors in the old days in Odessa. My parents had operated an inn where travelers stopped for a night's lodging, or a vodka or schnapps. The government sent these inspectors out to the ghetto to collect heavy taxes, arbitrarily assessed, from those Jews who reaped even a small profit from their work. The village people often called on Papa to intercede on their behalf. According to Mama, he could outtalk and outmaneuver the inspectors every time. He would give them a hearty welcome and regale them with long stories, all the while loading them with liquor until, tipsy and sleepy, they had to stay for the night. In the morning, instead of collecting fines from Papa, they paid him off not to report their conduct.

Sometimes, however, his jokes were not so funny. To find out whether or not the Santa Claus we heard about from other children was real, we put our stockings on the mantelpiece one Christmas Eve. In the night my father filled them with charcoal and stale bread and, the next morning, roared with laughter at our bitter discovery. How nasty, we thought, to take pleasure in our disillusionment.

In appearance and temperament Mother was his complete opposite. They were, in fact, totally unsuited to each other. Their marriage had been arranged by a *chatchan,* or marriage broker. Mother stood just under five feet. Her lean, muscular body declared her industry and dignity. She had a long, thin face, high cheekbones, large gray eyes (her outstanding feature, according to my sisters), and long, wavy black hair, which she parted in the middle and twisted into a bun in the back.

Cooking, scrubbing, sitting on a stool while washing a heaping tub of clothes singing Russian folksongs—these are the ways I remember her, these and her faith and optimism.

"You'll have everything you need when you grow up," she would say.

"Mom, how do you know? What makes you say that?"

"I know you will. I'm positive. You'll see."

I was still unconvinced. How could she say, "I know you will," when, as far as I could see, life was always going to be hard.

She took her turn in line every Tuesday at 7:00 A.M. to receive the fifty-pound burlap sacks of coal that were dispensed to the poor people by the city. How her tiny frame managed to lug them home, or how she withstood zero weather, sometimes blizzards, none of us ever figured out. Her complete lack of concern for her own comfort or convenience annoyed us.

"Why don't you make him haul the coal?" we pleaded with her. But no, Papa had to be waited on—it was her lot. To stretch the pennies far enough to feed the family meat and vegetables, she herself had coffee or tea with roll and butter three times a day. In those days you could get quantities of barley, beans, parsnips, parsley, carrots, onions, celery, and soup greens for a dime. The steaming tureens of vegetable soup made many delicious and nourishing meals. Whether it was kasha, blintzes, noodle charlotte, or a compote of stewed prunes and apricots, her cooking was of that exquisite flavor that only love and intuition can achieve.

She never took to her bed when she was ill. To cure the flu she did a day's washing and scrubbed the floors. Except for the birth of her babies, the only time Mother spent in a hospital was for a week's treatment for foot infection. The nurses could not make her understand that she was a patient. She would rise before anyone else stirred each morning, tidy up the room, make her bed, and when the attendant or nurse appeared, ask what she could do to help. When they reprimanded her for being on that foot and tried to put her to bed again, she would say, "But I feel fine."

From the old country Mother had brought with her many superstitions. When I came home from school one day with a rash on my face she said, "People complimented you too much. Too much praise brings bad luck. It's a *connahorrah,* a 'hex.' "

A petticoat or stocking put on inside out meant you would have a surprise that day, and tea leaves in a cup meant you would be receiving a letter or a package. And Mother cynically warned, "Sing before noon, cry pretty soon."

In our family religion was a free-floating affair. Although we children went to Sunday school, the Old Testament stories washed over us like a cosmic form of the Brothers Grimm or Hans Christian Andersen. But religion was a comfort to my parents, the only real comfort they ever had. They were sure that, in some mysterious way, life would work out according to God's purposes and that ultimately these were good. God was never far away. We often heard expressions such as "If only God will spare me," "God forbid," "Thank God," or "Only God knows." At Yom Kippur Mother fasted twenty-four hours. At Passover there was a special set of dishes, and we ate matzoh instead of bread. Such holidays were the only times the entire family sat down to a meal together.

On high holy days Papa went to the synagogue. Not Mother. She felt she could pay God her respects wherever she was. Mother lit candles on Friday night, and a *yahrzeit* candle once a year. She never put it into words, but from her day-to-day living, we knew her beliefs: that man best serves God by serving man, that work cures everything, that self is meant to be lost in something bigger, and that cleanliness is next to godliness.

She regarded death as a passing from one stage to another—part of a process in the total plan, quite acceptable in her sight.

One summer a seven-year-old playmate of mine on our block died of polio.

"Mama," I said, "dying means the end of everything, doesn't it? Why should Lillian be taken away? She was a nice girl."

Said Mother, "Maybe it would have been harder for her if she had lived. Dying isn't hard for the people who die. It's just hard for those who are left. I'm not afraid to die. I'm ready whenever God wants me."

The night after that discussion, I lay in bed shuddering at the thought of being lowered into the ground in a wooden box. How would they know you were really dead? Strange way to go to God, I thought.

She was equally philosophical about the vicissitudes of life, coping, without complaint or panic, with whatever fate handed her.

Sarah, first of the American-born children, was an example of what often happened, in those days, as the result of too late diagnosis. A midwife ushered her into the world and let her drop out of her crib shortly afterwards. The fall, we realized some ten or twelve years later, left her with impaired hearing and coordination. We thought of her as just "nervous." Today they would call her "athetoid." But unlike Becky or Jean, Sarah made friends easily and helped Mother with sewing, shopping, and cooking throughout her life.

My parents knew only approximately the year each of us was born; neither of them knew the exact day. I was told that I had been born on Thanksgiving. Fortunately, school authorities were able to shed light on the problem by writing to the Board of Health.

To escape Papa's sullen moods and temper tantrums, all eight children left home as soon as possible, most of them jumping into marriage in their teens. Fanny, the eldest, eloped at sixteen. Marriage rescued Ida from work in a tin-foil factory when she had barely turned seventeen.

At thirteen Dave started work, carrying heavy bundles of thread to the garment factories downtown. His pay was five dollars a week. When his route was longer than twenty blocks, he got a nickel for carfare. He stayed out late one night; Papa was furious and locked him out. The next day he packed and left. In time he progressed from messenger, to salesman, to buyer in a stationery firm. He eventually formed a successful partnership with a printer. After a third try with Gertrude, he stayed happily married.

The most colorful of the Russian-born four was Nathan. He was home during the day, so we assumed he had a nighttime job. It was only years later that we learned from Dave what was really going on.

"He went to school," Dave said, "but came right out

My Family

again. I don't know why Papa never locked him out—maybe he knew he was making money. We used to share the same cot and when he got home, usually around three in the morning, he just shoved me against the wall and kept me awake the rest of the night with his snoring. It wasn't until I got out of the house that I found out what was going on. He was accepting bets from all over the country: bets on baseball, fights, horses, anything. He got to be a big operator—it ran into the thousands. He really got into this racket when he started going with May—called himself a 'commission broker.' Her family lent him five thousand dollars to put him into the big-time bookie business. Sig, as they called him, was a shrewd operator. Don't sell him short. One time a customer couldn't pay him off. Nathan, knowing the man owned the Century Apartments on Fifty-ninth Street and Central Park West, settled for a rent-free apartment in the customer's building, a Cadillac, and a chauffeur, instead of cash. This chauffeur was a strong-arm guy, that's what I think. He must have been good as a protector, because there isn't a bookie alive who hasn't enemies, and Nathan was no exception. Oh, he knew Rosenthal, Gyp the Blood, Baby-Face Nelson—all of the big boys. For a while Nathan used a hearse garage as a blind for his bookie business. And then he met the boys, and did a lot of business at the Café Royal on Twelfth Street at Second Avenue—that was the night work."

At the time, none of us had any understanding of his underworld activities, although we suspected his involvement in some dark exploit remote from the family.

My only recollection of Nathan is of the one or two visits he made every year with his wife, May. On these occasions the atmosphere was grim. There was never any warning when they would come. They would just arrive and sit.

Nathan spoke softly, in a flat, metallic tone, and in short, clipped questions rather than sentences:

"How ya gettin' along, Rose?"

"What's new?"

"How are the kids?"

Never any real conversation.

Mother would ask, "How are you?"

The answer: "Fine."

Long pause.

Mother, trying again: "How's everything?"

Nathan: "Fine."

Another silence.

Mother: "Come and eat something. I have some potato pancakes."

Nathan: "No, we just ate."

After twenty minutes of looking at each other and uttering a syllable or two, Nathan would say, "Well, Ma, we have to go. Take care." And he would slip her some money and be gone for another year.

He loathed Papa, but for Mother's sake Nathan sent money home to help with the rent for as long as times were good with him. Eventually things got hot for Nathan, and whether it was twinges of conscience or the cops' closing in, he quit the brotherhood and found a safer life as the owner of a cigar store.

Those duty calls puzzled and saddened me. They were obviously just token visits—Nathan felt he ought to come and see his mother once in a while. And Mother surprised me by not probing beneath the surface to ask what he was doing with his life. Again she must have suppressed her own feelings rather than incur his displeasure. Another case of covering up. I decided that a lot of living happened on two planes: one inside you, the other to show the world.

[2]

Just One of Her Eight

WHEN I WAS two years old, Sarah, Jean, Becky, and I had the measles. They made a quick recovery, but the neighbors, hearing that I was still ill and that the condition was contagious, reported it to the Board of Health. An official came to the house and ordered me sent to Bellevue Hospital.

There, on a gray afternoon in 1918, my parents heard the verdict:

"Your baby is going blind. Congenital glaucoma—eventually she will see only light and shadow. No cure."

Tears gushed from my mother's eyes. My father choked back his. But neither fully understood the implications of the diagnosis, because in the examining room I had correctly pointed right, left, up, or down at the doctor's testing light. I was still their blue-eyed,

Just One of Her Eight

blond-haired two-year-old, using my eyes—as far as they could tell—entirely normally. Adversity was an old acquaintance, a traveler who had once knocked at their door, been admitted, and never left. They had lived with misfortune; somehow they would cope with this.

Deeply shocked as Mother must have been, she never felt any of the fear, guilt, shame, or resentment with which many parents react to the realization that they have an incurably blind child. Mother treated me as just one of her eight children. As she had with Sarah's mishap, Mother accepted mine as part of the texture of life. In fact, not until I was five years old did I discover that anyone regarded me as different from other children.

In the candy store across from where we lived, I stood at the counter one day, waiting for my licorice and jelly beans. As the shopkeeper slipped them into the bag, I overheard him whisper to the lady next to me, "Such a pretty child—isn't it terrible she's blind."

I can still feel the blood rush to my face and the sting of embarrassment. I dashed home and into the kitchen where Mama was ironing.

"Mama, Mama," I sobbed, "the candy man said it's terrible to be blind. Is it, Mama, is it?"

"Don't believe him," she said angrily, putting a firm hand on my shoulder, then sitting down and taking me on her lap.

"It isn't terrible. You wake up every morning with a smile on your face. You make your own bed. You run by yourself. You play with the other children. Don't believe him, *dolla meine*."

It hurt to know that anyone felt sorry for me. Certainly no one in the family and none of the kids on the block ever did.

Mama was comforting to a degree, but I knew in my heart that the candy man was not altogether wrong. The proof came from—of all people—my father.

Mother had been out helping a sick neighbor one afternoon and was late in starting the fire in the big coal stove. That meant supper would be late, and Papa would be angry. When the front door opened I hid in the bedroom. Pretty soon I heard him shouting.

"What's there to eat, crazy woman? Why isn't my supper on the table?"

The next sounds were blows—he was beating Mother. I ran into the kitchen and screamed, "Stop that!"

He turned on me. "Be quiet, blind animal!"

Suddenly the fear I had always had of him swelled and boiled into hate.

"It's you who are an animal. You're ashamed because I'm blind." I ran to the fire-escape window and called out, "Mrs. Stern, Mrs. Stern," but there was no answer. I listened. He had heard me. The blows stopped. It would be many years before the scalding memory of that scene cooled.

There were other childhood terrors. I was sitting in a friend's kitchen one morning when an animal leaped into my lap. A scream stuck in my throat. My flesh crawled. I had known of nothing in the room—nothing that moved. It took a few seconds, perhaps minutes, before my heart stopped pounding enough to recognize from the claws that it was a cat. I recoiled—I could not touch it.

For years afterward I had recurring nightmares of cats in bed with me, crawling and scratching up my legs, arms, and face. Not until I was grown did the nightmares cease.

Every now and then some scholar does research on how blind people dream. If, like me, a blind person cannot remember seeing, her perceptions are of size, texture, form, sounds, spatial relations, movement—reflections of experiences she has had when awake. Events and emotions occur very much as they have been experienced consciously. I hear a friend's voice; I feel the material of her sleeve as I hold her arm. I am riding in a car, sensing the motion, hearing the motor. Sometimes I have the usual sensations of falling, falling. As with anyone else, episodes can have little connection—the dentist is filling my tooth in the middle of the supermarket.

For a long time in my dreams I was chased by drunks trying to grab me. It all started with the janitors of our old tenement house, Eddie and Hugh, brothers who lived in the basement. I was sitting on our stoop one day when I heard them coming. They were making bloodcurdling sounds. Eddie was in his usual drunken stupor, belching and retching. I could smell the urine in his pants. Hugh, a deaf-mute whom the kids called "dummy," accompanied his sign language with vocal aberrations, apparently trying to communicate something to his brother. Terrified, I jumped up, rang our bell—it seemed hours before it was answered—and fled inside. I grew up with a visceral fear of drunks.

Between the time I was two and five, sight imperceptibly slipped away, leaving me able to see light, shadows, and for a few years and at close range, color. I learned to perceive the objective world through sound, touch, smells, relationships. It was an instinctive process. I learned to identify people by their voices; a flower by its form, texture, and fragrance. By the bounce or echo of sounds against the walls of a room I could tell its approximate size and the height of the ceiling. I memorized my way from one place to another, using echoes and resonances to correct veering in walking and to distinguish open space from closed-in areas. Familiar as I became with our block, I could easily judge where to turn in for the shoemaker across the street, or to meet a playmate two doors to the right of our house. From habit and the remembrance of the space relationships, I could run in from the street, down a long, narrow hall and stop exactly in front of the door of our flat.

Most of what my family saw from the window, I discerned by sound: Tinny tunes heralded the organ grinder; the wail "rags, bottles, sacks," the peddler; and often in those days one heard "clip clop" of horses' hooves, and wagons jouncing along the gutters. Now and then we were treated to oom-pa-pa German bands that played in the streets for pennies.

I distinguished clothes by touch. My black shoes had laces, the white ones, buttons. My blue skirt was straight and was made of wool; the black one was of silk and was pleated. The family was fanatical about appearance: It wasn't enough to be clean, you had to look scrubbed. Mother washed, starched, and ironed everything we wore every day. From the talk around me I learned what people looked like, what was meant by a tailored dress or coat, what colors went well together, which materials were transparent, what styles were in the best taste—simple lines, according to Mother—and much other visual information.

In the early twenties the New York streets were happy playgrounds. On the sidewalk in front of our tenement we jumped rope—high-low water—to see how high we could jump. Sometimes we competed to see who could jump off the highest stoop.

Stella from up the block joined us occasionally. She was a lanky, freckle-faced tomboy with long legs, a bony frame, and a vivid imagination. She was deep in the Claude Lightfoot books. I was Henry Archer, the quarterback, and she, of course, was Lightfoot, the captain. I found out about the bony frame when she made us all practice tackling. When someone got a nosebleed or a bruised leg, she would say, "That's nothing. You only get hurt when you're good. Don't be a sissy."

There were wonderful games: Red Rover, Red Rover, Let Sadie Come Over; Crack the Whip; Spin the Bottle; and Simon Says. On roller skates we played Tally-Ho, the daredevils in the gang hitching onto automobiles for a ride to the opposite end of the street. As a Sunday special, one of the more affluent neighbors would treat some of us to rides on the ponies in Central Park.

Sometimes Jean and I joined other children in a game of tag on the nearby East River pier. Once I collided with a post and came home with a gash that required six stitches in the right corner of my forehead. Jean got a spanking, not for letting me play tag, but for failing to warn me that there was a post in my way.

We loved to sing and dance. At the corner store you could get sheets with the words of popular songs. We sang them together in harmony. We would turn on the radio in the dining room and Charleston, fox trot, and waltz with each other, trying to avoid the big round table. We competed in tricks: standing on our heads, doing the splits, cartwheeling, and somersaulting.

"Let's see you stand up, bend back till your head touches the floor."

"Let's see who can kick the highest—no good, Rose, that doesn't count; you have to point your toes and keep the other knee straight."

Blue-eyed, auburn-haired Jean, two years older than I, was the sister with whom I spent the most time. She was moody, but when she promised to do something you could count on her to keep her word. She was the most outrageously critical and bossy of the lot, but we took it from her because we knew she had our interests at heart. She set the standards for our clothes, hairdos, house furnishings. She never suggested—she made pronouncements. Somehow we met her specifications.

"God, aren't you ever going to change that hairdo—you need a cut." And cut it soon was. No one dared wear a pair of shoes after Jean had declared them ready for the ragbag. When she announced that we needed new curtains, somehow those curtains got changed.

She had a passion for throwing things out. One time she collected a large set of dishes. "These things are horrible, full of chips. We've got enough junk around here." Crash! Down the chute they went—cups, saucers, glasses, bowls.

She was the only one who stood up to Papa. He had a habit of sending her out for the evening papers, dailies he devoured after dinner. Finally one night she rebelled.

"I've been on my feet working in your shop all day. You pick them up on your way home."

He never again sent her on the errand.

Mother thoroughly spoiled Becky, her youngest. Everything, including ribbons and belts, had to be washed and ironed after one wearing. Becky had copper-colored hair, a peaches-and-cream complexion, and the best posture of all of us. She was limber and graceful. I wanted her to be a dancer, but I soon learned that my advice was the last thing in the world she would follow.

From the time I was four they took me with them to the movies. The Nickelodeon was only a block and a half from our house. Movies were silent then, and for me, a painful bore, but it was a way of getting out of the house. The girls were too engrossed to fill me in on what was going on, so I amused myself by listening to the piano-player. In time I recognized musical clues: The galloping theme from the *William Tell* Overture meant the posse was giving chase; an ominous, rising theme in a minor key got a hiss or a boo from the audience—enter the villain; "Hearts and Flowers," in tremolo rendition, something sad. Comedies were the worst to sit through. Hearing the audience roar at Charlie Chaplin without knowing what it was all about made me feel stupid and left-out, like a deaf person in the presence of a conversation in which he cannot take part.

Somehow, despite romps with my sisters and playmates, and games in the street, time hung heavy in those early childhood days. There was never enough to do.

I remember plaguing Mother with, "What can I do now—what can I do now?" We couldn't afford toys, and dolls were a total bore. There were never any books in the house, nor was there anyone to read them to me if there had been. So it was a great joy when I was old enough to start school.

[3]

Gateway to a Seeing World

EVERYONE WAS a bit fluttery that morning—my first day of school. More hurriedly than usual, Mother bathed me in the washtub, washed and combed my hair—worn parted in the center with long corkscrew curls—and dressed me in a stiffly starched white middy blouse and blue pleated skirt.

As usual, conversation was minimal, the family straggling in one or two at a time. When I sat down to breakfast, Sarah and Becky were squabbling over a hair ribbon both wanted to wear, Papa was skimming the morning paper, and Jean was finishing her coffee.

Much as I longed to go to school, the thought of boarding at a school for the blind, recommended by a neighbor, was frightening. I had been playing with the kids on the street—why now did I have to be sent away?

"Jean, why can't I go to your school?" I asked.

" 'Cause you have to go to a special school to learn how to read."

"But not to come home except for weekends—" The tears started to flow.

"Don't worry, Rozola," Mother said. "You'll like it. You'll meet new children, they'll teach you to read, and you'll be busy all day like you always want to be."

"Hurry, hurry," interrupted Papa. "We have to take a trolley across town and walk twelve blocks to that place. Finish up."

He put down the paper, rose quickly, and then, after helping me on with my heavy coat and my wool tam-o'-shanter, dampened a clothes brush and vigorously brushed me off.

"Be careful," Mother called out, as we left, and turned to attack the daily stack of washing.

After we got off the trolleycar, Papa hurried me along until I was out of breath.

"We're almost there," he said. "It's across the—" He stopped dead in his tracks, whirled around and started back the way we had come.

"What's the matter, Papa?"

"Never mind. Not for you."

What a relief! I didn't care what he didn't like or what was wrong.

Mother was equally confused to see us back so soon.

"What happened?"

"That's a terrible place. We didn't even go in. Can you imagine? Bars on all the windows. It's a prison, not a school."

"But what will we do?" Mother asked frantically. "She must go to school."

"She'll go. She'll go. Don't get excited. Maybe they'll take her at Jean's school."

To everyone's relief, P.S. 17 did indeed accept blind children. I could go to and come home from school each day with Jean.

I have always been grateful to my father for saving me from a residential school. Separated from sighted children, I might have developed a fear and suspicion of seeing people that inhibits many graduates of schools for the blind. I might have grown up feeling completely comfortable only with other blind people.

At P.S. 17, as at certain other schools in New York, blind students attended regular classes, reporting to their special rooms during recess, lunch, and study periods. There the Braille teacher assisted with transcriptions into Braille of blackboard material, examination questions, and reading assignments. She also interlined in ink, for grading by the regular teacher, tests that we had Brailled in class.

Soon the New York Public Library began sending me huge Braille books. They started with twenty-one tomes of the Bible, of all things. They kept coming and coming, and I kept plowing through each one, confused by the begats, bored by the battles, not understanding how God could make the whole world in six days, and appalled at the slaying of fatted calves for the great Jehovah. After all, the calves were part of his precious flock, too. Happily, *Heidi, Anne of Green Gables, Lorna Doone, The Prince and the Pauper,* and *Hans Brinker, or, The Silver Skates* followed. They came with me to the table, to streetcars (until my sisters protested because people stared at me), and to bed.

When I was in the seventh grade Papa moved the family and his store uptown and transferred me to P.S. 54 and to the most vividly remembered of my Braille teachers, Bessie Bluman. Her voice and laughter were a delight. She was straight and true with us, praising sparingly. We respected her the more for it.

When you entered her room you might find a girl "seeing" with her fingers the shape of the earth and the location of countries and continents on the large globe that stood by the windows. Its smooth surfaces represented water; the raised areas, land masses; and those raised still more, mountains. If you happened to arrive at recess, you might find a boy turning somersaults over the parallel bars at the back of the room. In the spring there would be lilacs, jonquils, or pussy willows in the garden corner, and always you would hear, mingled with the learning, lively talk and laughter.

Up front were stacks of Braille books and maps, piled on long shelves. We sat at washtublike desks, practical for storing Braille slates and paper.

We were a motley class, but Miss Bluman managed somehow to encourage whatever abilities she observed. Pete, who beat me at chinning the bar and broad jumps, was clever at handwork. Miss Bluman taught him how to make a Braille ruler. She gave him a long stick, sandpaper, a hammer, and the twelve tacks to be spaced an inch apart.

Bessie Bluman taught us to sit up straight. "Keep your head up. Show your pretty face and look at the person you are talking to."

She taught us to find things and put them away independently, to say "Please" and "Thank you." She corrected a nervous habit I had of pulling at my curls and letting them spring back.

"You can't take credit for your hair," she pointed out. "God gave you that."

She made us figure arithmetic in our heads and memorize poetry. During lunch she played Galli-Curci, Caruso, and Ponselle records, discussing their roles and telling us the plots of the operas.

Bessie Bluman took us to the Museum of Natural History and the Metropolitan Museum of Art. The authorities gave blind children special permission to touch sculpture, bas-reliefs, carved sarcophagi, animals of wood and stone, pottery, fabrics, basketry, and armor. By touch we learned to recognize the smooth, cold hardness of marble, the living quality of wood, the sturdy richness of bronze, the heavy roughness of stone. We saw furrowed brows, tough leg muscles, graceful embracings, the forward thrust of figures in motion. We learned how in modern art a single curved line might symbolize a bird, an assemblage—anything.

These excursions to the museums illuminated our understanding of ancient cultures and showed us how to use them to enlarge our knowledge of the objective world. They made us realize how important it was then, and always would be, for those who could not see the world with their eyes to take every opportunity possible to touch things. Visitors came to observe and to learn from Bessie Bluman. One day while we were demonstrating our ability to read Braille, we overheard one of them say, "Doesn't your heart ache for these children? Don't you find it hard being with them all day?"

"Not at all," Miss Bluman answered in her clear,

forthright voice. "I completely forget that they can't see. To me they are just children. I love my work."

And we loved her.

But Bessie Bluman and public school were not the only good fortune of New York's blind children in those days. There was that place on Fifty-ninth Street near Park Avenue, the New York Association for the Blind. The present Lighthouse is a fourteen-story monolith on the same site, but the old building, dating back to 1911, was a ramshackle wooden affair. There were business offices on the mezzanine. On the second floor, fifty or more blind women sat at looms or sewing machines; others made reed and raffia baskets. Administration offices were on the third floor, music rooms on the fourth, and the recreation department, with clubrooms, dining room, kitchen and office, on the fifth.

The director of recreation was the history-making pioneer, Alma I. Guy. She was a short, stocky woman with prominent teeth, high cheekbones, gray hair drawn straight back in a knot, and (as we found out from big hugs) large pendulous breasts. Heavy glasses corrected her own limited vision. She always carried a carpet-textured drawstring bag full of jingling loose change, which she used to pay the "guides" who called for the children at their homes and returned them after the day's activities. She was a tremendous influence on the lives of all who knew her, especially her "girls," as she called Chip, Pill, Polly, and me.

Quiet-spoken Chip, of tiny build, had a love of adventure and a magnetic personality. Of the group, she was the most gentle and tolerant. Although she couldn't see a jot of light, her uncanny sense of direction enabled her to bounce around with accuracy and speed. She had the sonar sense of a dolphin. Unlike the rest of us, she never said bad things about people. She played the piano beautifully and began teaching me some of her simpler pieces.

Pill was of medium height, with heavy bobbed hair and normal-looking eyes. Voluble, gregarious, and impulsive, she too was always ready for a lark. Like Chip, she was an independent spirit. Pill often took me home with her. She was studying the violin at the time. She said it was much harder to play than the piano because you had to make your own tone—and she really proved it. That fiddle of hers set my teeth on edge like the scratch of chalk on the blackboard. I made it sound worse, I am sure, by trying to improvise accompaniments to some of her solos.

After school, Pill, Chip, and I would set off on walks, banging into poles and people and giggling hysterically at a remark we heard more than once: "Whatsamadda? Cantcha see where yer goin'?"

Tall, tomboyish Polly had just enough vision to travel about independently. She complained that totally blind people were more fortunate because they were offered help. One day I asked her, "Would you rather have no vision at all? How would you like to change places with us?"

Silence.

"That's what I thought," I said.

One of our other Lighthouse pals left us with the only sad memory of those days. Mimi Baker was a tomboy who had never known a father and whose mother had to work to support the family. Early in her teens, Mimi began running around with boys on her block and, when she became visibly pregnant, the Lighthouse authorities banned her from all activities. We were shocked at this rejection and thought it had much to do with her ultimate fate: She ended up a beggar on the streets of New York.

Saturday was our big day. We started as Chickadees, then became Bluebirds and Campfire Girls. I remember our fascination with the fringed Indian costumes and the Campfire rings and beads each of us had to earn. Then there was a popular cooking class, in which we mainly pulled taffy, stirred and devoured fudge, gorged on nuts and raisins intended for cookies.

We learned to roller-skate on the Lighthouse roof. Until we got used to the skates, we held on to a metal bar circling an enclosure at one end. We played wild games: musical chairs, tug-of-war, relay races, and hide-and-seek over the five floors, sliding down banisters, crouching under desks, squeezing into cupboards between jars of peanut butter and crockery.

Other Lighthouse children, overprotected at home, had less fun. Etta, aged nine, obese and with greasy curls that smelled like stale butter, would not stir from her chair until someone came along and took her by the hand. Maggie, aged eleven, whined constantly and needed help in using her knife and fork. Carol, at thirteen, admitted that her mother always laced her shoes and buttoned her dresses.

Miss Guy put a quick stop to all that, as she did to our habits of rocking back and forth and sticking fingers in our eyes—mannerisms of blind children from lack of activity and visual stimulus. She would often come up behind us and straighten our shoulders or tap us gently on the tops of our heads.

"Up, up!" she would insist. "Let's sit up tall and proud. Only puppies' chests face the floor—there, that's so much better." For the worst offenders, like me, she arranged corrective gymnastics. I abhorred the contraption which clamped around my head and pulled me some two feet up in the air where I dangled painfully, in perfect posture.

Miss Guy often held me on her lap, smoothing my hair and straightening my ribbons. Taking my hands, she would clap them together in rhythm to the tune of "Pease Porridge Hot," or her favorite, "Where Oh Where Has My Little Dog Gone"—all totally off key. Often I got a ride on her knees to "Rosy, Posy, Puddin' 'n' Pie, Kissed the Boys and Made Them Cry."

The Lighthouse was a magnet for people interested in exploring new ideas for blind children. Edith Ballinger Price, a writer and illustrator of juvenile fiction, came by one Saturday and said she wanted to teach us about art. Weird idea, we thought—blind kids drawing? But "Prof" intrigued us. She was very tall, and she spoke in a low, rich, faraway voice.

"It's not drawing I want to teach you," she explained. "I just thought you girls would like to know how sighted people visualize and draw things."

At our first art session, Prof handed us a diagram she had pricked out on thick paper with a dressmaker's wheel and asked us to identify it. We said it looked like a semicircle with a loop at one end.

"That's a teacup," she said. "We draw just its outline because that's the way we see it." We were amazed.

This was a complete revelation to us! We had pictured it always as it felt to the touch—in its entirety, the whole cup and handle. Prof talked about the "limitations of sight," pointing out for example, that a cylinder can appear to the eye as a disc, whereas it is always a cylinder to the touch.

Her brother, Major Bill, an automotive engineer, devised an ingenious way to help us understand perspective. He set two wires on a board five inches apart, slanting them closer and closer until at the end of the board they nearly touched—the vanishing point.

"The farther away things are viewed," he explained, "the smaller they look."

We often met at his workshop, where he showed us the properties of mercury, the ductility of glass, and Morse code. He improvised buzzers so we could practice sending messages.

Then there was Molly Lingg, our Bluebird leader, who gave me a memorable week at her house in Midland Beach. It was my first experience at the ocean. The feeling of space, the salt air, the soft sand, the sound of the waves were strange and wonderful. Dashing into the surf, Molly and I rode the breakers back to the beach, tingling with the cold salt spray. We gathered shells, and Molly showed me how to listen for the echoes of the sea. She described how they had once housed living things and how you could tell crabs and clams and snails by their shape and texture. Barefoot, we ran along the hard, wet sand, hand in hand at first, then parting to see who could run the fastest. We jumped over seaweed and driftwood cast up by the tides, and with the sighted children on the beach, we played leapfrog and sculptured each other's hands and feet in the sand.

And the Lingg house—that was how rich people lived! There was an upstairs, and each person had her own room and her own bed. I noticed that Molly and her two sisters sat down together at mealtimes. How peaceful and orderly compared to home.

"Goldilocks, it looks as though another fairy's come visiting this morning," Molly said. There by my breakfast plate would be a charm bracelet, a coral necklace, a coin purse, ribbons, or a music box. Soon we were off to the playground for rides on a pony, a carousel, a seesaw, or, best of all, a swing. It felt like flying—I would sit or stand in it and Molly would push me higher and higher. I wanted to stay at Midland Beach forever.

Home would have been a miserable letdown had it not been for another magical event.

One day the Lighthouse director, Mr. Scandlin, called me into his office.

"I hear you like to pick up tunes on the piano?"

"Yes, I do," I said.

"How would you like to take piano lessons?"

"Oh, I would! I would, very much," I said eagerly. "But we have no piano."

"Well, Rose, a Lighthouse friend who will never need it again has willed her piano to you."

The following week they moved a square white grand piano, minus many ivories, into our front room. It was so huge that it barely left enough space for the stool. I was beside myself with joy—a piano! A big piano! It was a miracle. I felt as though I had acquired not just an instrument but a whole new world of my own. And such, indeed, it proved to be.

My piano teacher Mary Keybler was a graduate of the Batavia School for the Blind and the New England Conservatory. A portly lady with a cheery voice, she steered me through scales and arpeggios, insisting on flat, motionless wrists, not caring how I held my fingers as long as they played the right notes.

I loved my piano, but I rarely practiced. I would quickly dispense with the week's assignment and drift into improvisations. I began experimenting with patterns of melody, harmony, and rhythm. In some strange way, the piano always picked up the tenor of my moods. Sometimes they were slow, languorous phrases in a minor key, sometimes quick, staccato fragments and big chords that felt good under my fingers. All the bad things—irritation, disappointment, loneliness—went away when I was at the piano.

Papa regarded my music as a complete waste of time.

"You'll never make any money playing the piano," he muttered.

But Mother thought it important. When I offered to help with the dishes, she would have none of it.

"No, no, you play. Some day you'll give a concert."

Once when I was at the piano and she at her washing as usual, she said, "Let's play a duet—I'm learning all your pieces on my washboard."

One night in a blizzard Mother took me on the old Second Avenue El to a concert at the Educational Alliance on Delancey Street. Bundled to the ears, with the icy wind howling around us, we trudged through the slippery streets, arriving with toes, fingers, and noses numb. But the discomfort vanished as we listened enthralled to the timbre and dialogue of instruments, the bright and dark harmony, the lusty and lilting rhythms of Haydn, Mozart, and Beethoven.

Along with crafts, cooking, art, and music, Alma Guy was responsible for the first dramatics group for blind children. Our first coach was Ida May Wilcox, a friend of Guy's, studying to be a kindergarten teacher at Columbia.

"You're going to love her," Miss Guy said. "She has blue eyes, dark hair, and a radiant personality. She's a kind of storybook person."

The moment we met her, all of us fell in love with Ida May. Her laugh was like wind bells stirring in a breeze.

She began by reading *Little Women* aloud. Two Saturdays later, when she had finished, she asked if we would like to act it out.

"Could we? Could we?" We clapped our hands and jumped up and down in our excitement.

"I'll be Jo."

"No, me."

Everyone wanted to play Jo. Polly was the lucky one. Chip played Beth, Pill played Meg, and I played Amy.

Some of the Lighthouse staff were afraid we would walk off the stage, but Ida May found a way to prevent that. She put down a rubber mat as a boundary we could recognize when our toes touched it. That calmed everybody, and the Lighthouse Players, as we were to be known, were launched.

We first read our parts, then walked through them onstage. Another mat, laid down to indicate direction, helped with tricky entrances and exits.

At first our motions, facial expressions, and gestures were awkward, constrained, rigid, lacking in feeling. Ida May realized that the seeing child acquires various modes of expression through imitation, unconsciously absorbed as everyday kinds of communication. As an infant, he sees his mother nod and smile with approval, sees her approach with a pointed finger meaning "naughty child," sees his schoolmates wave hello and goodbye. A shrug of the shoulders means "I don't know" or "I don't care." Ida May had to teach us to look toward the person we were talking to, raise an eyebrow to express doubt, nod in agreement, and use all the gestures commonly used by sighted people.

Dramatics ushered us into a wider and more vivid world—the magic of makeup, the flurry of dress rehearsal, the crisis of opening night. We learned about foreign customs by maneuvering heavy Spanish furniture, climbing into fourposter beds, and managing our crinoline skirts, stiff collars, and Napoleonic uniforms. We learned about French provincial interiors and the crude furnishings of an Irish cottage by the sea.

There was the glamour of meeting people in the literary and theatrical world. For five seasons the Lighthouse Players gave Saturday matinees at the Booth Theater on Broadway. Billie Burke supplied costumes from the Ziegfeld chorus wardrobe. Myrna Loy, Loretta Young, Otis Skinner, and George Arliss came to see our performances. Chip and Pill performed with Walter Hampden in a one-act play. He even entertained them afterwards at his home in Ridgefield, Connecticut.

Over the years, the Players accumulated an assortment of men—single, married, widowed, elderly—who, under the guise of theater patrons, saw us as likely subjects for a bit of amorous dalliance. Dr. Dickie, a widower in his eighties, gave each of us a turn at interminable phone conversations in which he offered gifts, dinners, and money as bait for a night at a swanky hotel.

"Rose," he would say, "can you come to dinner with

me tomorrow night? I haven't seen you for quite a while, you know. I won't keep you long."

Because he was a major Lighthouse patron, we compromised by going to tea with him, inveigling one of our pals along whenever possible. For reasons we soon recognized, he would insist on a place with curtained booths so that after the waitress brought our order he could wriggle up close and get his hands first around our waists, then under our skirts. He had the soft, pudgy hands of a man who lived a soft, pudgy life. When one of us pushed him away, he would behave, but not for long. Soon under one or the other's skirt would go the hands. He smelled of rancid sweat. The old codger repelled and disgusted us. In time we had the courage to refuse him and hung up when he called.

We came to know the gifts and foibles of directors, their struggles to appease all contenders for the star roles. We came to know the suspense of audience reaction, the gratification of laughter, applause, silence, and intangibles felt across the footlights.

The first play we performed on Broadway was *The Toy Shop,* produced at the Lyceum Theater. As far as I can recall, none of us had the slightest concept of the glamour of a Broadway debut. When we arrived at the theater, the magnitude of the occasion hit us and sent us spinning into a wild hubbub—the size of the stage, the footlights, the private dressing rooms, the bustling stagehands.

When the curtain went up I was lying across the knees of Tackhammer, the toymaker. He was stitching me up the back, as he sang, "I'm Tackhammer, the toymaker, the jolly old man . . ." Coming to life, I slowly rose from his knees, faced the audience, and clutching my stomach and bending over and back as though in acute pain, sang in my child's treble:

> I've got a pain in my sawdust,
> That's what's the matter with me.
> Something is wrong with my little insides,
> I'm just as sick as can be.
>
> Someone please run for the medicine man,
> Someone else fetch me a fan,
> Everyone hurry as fast as you can
> 'Cause I've got a pain in my sawdust.

We discovered that no amount of rehearsing guaranteed a flawless performance. In *Pickaro Amour,* Chip and I somehow missed the tiny opening backstage through which we were to exit. We floundered and fumbled along the backdrop and finally, doubled up in uncontrollable giggles, crawled off under the curtain. And none too soon, because Chip wet her pants.

I had a moment of mortification in the production of the one-act play "Sintram of Skagerrak," in which I played the lead. Sintram, a tubercular poet, falls madly in love with the sea. The set was a beaverboard spiral built up to about six feet to give the impression of high cliffs at the ocean's edge. At the end of the play, Sintram stands on the cliff and calls, "Ah, Beloved—at last!" thereupon plunging into its depths.

A leap from the precipice should have been followed by a great splashing sound. Instead, the audience heard, quite distinctly, the dull thud of me, landing on a soft mattress. The sound man had forgotten his cue. My dramatic exit was ruined.

Whether we performed one- or three-act plays—fantasy, mystery, farce, or tragedy—at a school, at a club, in a hotel, or on Broadway—we worked hard to meet the high standards of performance set by all our directors. These experiences helped immeasurably to enhance our pleasure in attending the theater.

Eventually, the Lighthouse replaced the old platform on which we had started with a huge stage, real curtains, footlights, spotlights, and a dressing room for each player. No Broadway theater exuded more glamour.

I wish that all blind children could have the opportunities Pill, Polly, Chip, and I had as children in the old New York days. I wish they could have the association and guidance of imaginative people like Bessie Bluman, Alma Guy, and Ida May Wilcox, that they could have the training in self-reliance, in athletics, dramatics, and some form of artistic expression. For blind children such training is paramount not only for physical, personal, and social development, but also for the ability to function with freedom, confidence, and happiness in their daily lives. Through such experiences they can expand their boundaries, cast off their shackles of inaction, be more nearly like other children, and grow up to be part of their communities with a larger share of life and living. For us, the Lighthouse was a gateway to the seeing world.

[4]

Mossyledge

Polly, Pill, Chip, and I spent the happiest of our childhood summers at Mossyledge, Ida May's camp on Lake Memphremagog in Georgeville, Quebec. The moment we stepped ashore we jumped up and down, waved our arms in the air, and shouted, "We're here, we're here!" as though we had just arrived in heaven.

The first time we went, in 1927, Polly was fifteen, Pill and Chip, thirteen, and I, eleven. Early in July we took a train to Newport, Vermont, then a motor launch up the lake past the Green Mountains. As we approached, Miss Guy spoke lovingly of the white birches along the rocky shore, and behind them, the pines and cedars.

"And from the wharf at camp, we look across to mountains that resemble their names: Owl's Head and Elephantis. Veteran campers climb them each year. Some day you may want to try them."

Ida May was at the dock to greet us.

"Bless your hearts, I thought you'd never come. Just leave the bags—Hugo and Mr. Hepburn will get them later. Guy, you look tired—working round the clock as usual, I suppose. Chip never changes. Pill, good—you've brought your fiddle. Polly, aren't you ever going to stop growing? Posy, we'll have to get some roses in those cheeks."

The sun burned brilliant. The air was crisp and full of evergreen smells. We gulped them in. As we quickly proceeded under their arches on the trail to the main cabin, I detected their shadows, playing tag with sharp pools of light.

A man-sized breakfast and roaring fire awaited us in the main cabin. We ate on the porch off the living room overlooking the lake. I remember the bee that stung me on the midriff after sampling the marmalade on my toast at breakfast; Ida May's incomparable bread, chicken pilaf, and maple ice cream; the grownups' awe at the coral sunsets; and the wild storms, with their thunderclaps and lightning that leaped at us, sometimes coming up quite suddenly from across the lake.

The main cabin, to the left of the boat dock, almost filled the only clearing in the area. Cedar-lined paths led to the dozen or more sleeping cabins in the woods. Ida May and her father had built them of logs, open on four sides with canvas curtains one could pull closed when it rained. There was no electricity, and the only running water, which had to be boiled for dishwashing, was in the kitchen. As a nightly ritual, each camper picked up a lamp, then filled a pail of water to take to his cabin for sponge baths out of a tin basin. The toilets were outside.

The guests were Ida May's friends. Hugo van Arks,

one of her unsuccessful suitors, edited a nautical magazine. Grace Boughton, an actress, alone much of the time, was a picture, Ida May said, as she paddled her canoe—standing up. Mr. Fitch, an authority on labor relations, and Mr. Hepburn, a Canadian minister, who taught us the Drummond songs, took us for long walks.

This first experience at living in the woods was sometimes terrifying to us city-dwellers. One time all of us sprang up out of a deep sleep—someone was slurping water out of the pail by Chip's bed. She reached out and screamed. Miss Guy came running over in her nightgown.

"It's only old Betsy wandering out of the cow barn. There's a full moon tonight and that does strange things to animals, and people, too, sometimes."

All too often she had to come to our cabin in the middle of the night to stop the noise. "You children simply must learn to conform," she would say sternly. "Think of other people. They've been working hard all day. You're keeping them awake with your prattling and giggling. Besides, you need to rest. Now go to sleep."

And quiet would reign for perhaps five minutes.

Each morning, Guy measured out doses of milk of magnesia for each of us. Sometime during every day, she rounded us up and made us sunbathe in our "birthday suits" while she read aloud to us.

"Lie down," she'd say. "I'd rather have you fall asleep than have you sit up round-shouldered."

The older campers taught us how to enjoy the wilderness. Hugo showed us how to blow musical notes through long grasses and reeds. He took us for rides in the rowboats. At first he did the rowing, but upon our insistence we ourselves took turns at the oars.

From Ida May we learned how to make pillows of pine needles, and birds' nests from birch bark, fern, and moss. A true child of nature, she knew where to find huckleberries and how to sip nectar from nasturtiums. She introduced us to the form and fragrance of water-lilies in a pond not far from camp. I remember the sweet, candylike smell of Queen Anne's lace; the prickly softness of buttercups; the singsong we intoned as we pulled petals—"He loves me, he loves me not"—not caring how it came out; the good-luck four-leaf clovers we found in the grass; and the big wooden swing we piled into after supper to listen for the last bird calls of the day.

Mr. Hepburn announced one night that our long walks were merely preparation for a fourteen-mile overnight hike to the foot of Owl's Head. We were flattered that he would take us along with some of the grownups, so the next morning, with knapsacks on our backs, Chip, Pill, and I each pairing off with one of the older people, set off at 7:00 A.M. The walk was the easiest part of the venture. When the heat of the day increased and our pace sagged, we struck up a marching rhythm: "Left, left, I had a good home and I left, right, right, right in the middle of a fight with my wife and forty-nine kids, left, left . . ." And so on. Toward noon, as we felt our packs weighing us down, we transferred the lunches from our backs to our stomachs. We stopped at every stream to quench our thirst.

But there was no relief from the agony of sleeping on the ground. In fact, I never did sleep. Leaves rustled, twigs snapped, animals prowled, owls hooted, and the katydid orchestra never ceased.

By morning, that infernal pebble under the spine felt

like a rock. Never was there more heavenly music than Mr. Hepburn's trumpet call of reveille. Amid the groans that came from those of us trying to put our knees, elbows, and necks back into place, a plaintive cry arose from one poor soul, apparently attempting to put on her shoes: "Has anyone got a shoehorn?"

After everyone had gone to bed one night, Miss Guy's girls remained fully dressed—we were in the mood for adventure. We found the path to the lake. The night was balmy and perfectly still, except for the chirp of a cricket and "bellunk" of a frog, a perfect night for a swim *au naturel*.

Leaving our clothes on a mound, we felt with our feet to the water's edge and waded in. When the water came up to our waists we started swimming.

"Gosh, isn't this delicious!" Pill squealed.

"It's so different without a suit," called out Chip. "Golly, I wonder if any boats ever get this way at night!"

Farther and farther out we swam, talking from time to time to be sure we kept together. Finally Chip said, "Hey kids, we'd better head back. Where in the world are we anyhow, Polly? Can you tell?"

"Nope—can't see a thing. I told you I'm just as blinky at night as you guys. By all means, turn around, everybody."

"Can't you just picture a search party finding us in the raw tomorrow morning!" I threw in.

Back we swam, standing now and then to test for depth until we thankfully arrived at the shallows. On shore we realized that the current had pulled us off course from where we had entered the water. Feeling hopelessly lost, we began hunting for our landmark. We kicked around, got down on all fours and groped for a while, then stood up again—two of us moving one way, two another—when suddenly Pill yelled, "Hey, come here—look what I found! A cornfield, for heaven's sake."

We caught up with her.

"Do you mean to say this has been here all this time and we never knew about it?" Chip commented disgustedly.

None of us had ever seen corn growing. We were astonished at its height. We each broke off an ear, peeled back the silk, and began biting into it. Then, to our horror, we heard footsteps. We plunged in among the stalks, crouched low, and huddled together. There we remained, holding our breaths, panicked. More thump-thumps, but now they sounded as though they were receding.

"Don't move yet," Chip whispered, "but I'll bet that was a raccoon. Don't you remember, Miss Guy told us they sound just like people walking."

Gradually we breathed again, rose cautiously, and extricated ourselves from the cornfield. Again we began stamping and kicking around in search of our clothes.

"Funny," remarked Pill, "you feel so much more naked when you walk then when you stand still. Hey," she went on, suddenly excited, "feel that breeze coming from our right? I'll bet we landed too far to the left. Let's try this way."

We followed her back past the cornfield some thirty yards—it felt like a mile—and practically fell over our precious mound.

"We aren't going to tell Guy about this, are we?" asked Polly. As the oldest, she always felt the most guilty.

"Gracious, no!" we all screamed. Chip reminded her,

"You're never, never supposed to go swimming without someone watching on shore."

Thus the days passed at Mossyledge, each one full to the brim. We walked to Georgeville for the mail three miles each way, swam a good part of the afternoon, and in the evening sat around the fire chatting, listening to someone reading aloud, or playing word games. Often the whole camp gathered around the piano and I would play for them to sing. Those were sparkling, carefree days with stories, music, fresh air, luscious food, and love all around us. Little did I realize that Mossyledge would one day be the model for another "fairyland of joy and beauty," as Guy called it, the blueprint of a dream for sightless children.

[5]

Transition

MAMA CONTINUED starching and ironing, Papa haranguing and erupting. He now demanded that she bring him hot lunches every day. This meant cooking in the morning as well as the afternoon and lugging heavy pots of food several blocks. He yanked Sarah out of school in the fourth grade, Jean in the seventh, to help him in the shop.

My sisters could count on a rampage whenever they got home after eleven o'clock at night: "Out with bums again! No decent fellow would keep a girl out so late."

Shortly after I had registered at Wadleigh High School, Papa's tailor shop burned to the ground. "We're moving to Brooklyn," he announced peremptorily.

Pill and Chip were now boarding at the Catholic Center in Manhattan for five dollars a week. Reluctant to change schools or quit the Players, I convinced Papa to let me stay there, too. We relished the sisters' homemade bread and loved to imitate their Irish brogues, but the rustle of their long robes and the rattle of their beads as they moved about the dining room and halls gave us an eerie feeling. Theaters, concerts, and Players rehearsals often kept us out till well past eleven o'clock. This created a thorny problem, since check-in time at the center was ten. Oh well, we thought, our room is right at the top of the staircase just inside the front door—we should be able to sneak in unnoticed.

No such thing. Sister Ambrose was always right there with a sharp reprimand: "Sorry, sorry—you're always sayin' you're sorry, but I never see any proof of it. Don't let this happen again."

Bells for prayers rang now and then. Most of the guests attended daily mass, so we decided that out of respect for the nuns we should show up at least once. But Sister Martha stopped Chip at the chapel door.

"My dear child," she said, aghast, "we can see your limbs. What kind of garment is that to wear to mass? You'd better be changin' it. It looks like a bathin' suit."

But the sisters were kind, and I felt fortunate to be away from the family dissension. When I was sixteen, Chip and Pill surprised me with my first birthday party. The nuns presented me with a Braille pocket watch in solid gold, with an "R" carved on the lid.

School, meanwhile, was very different from the halcyon days of P.S. 54. There were few texts in Braille, and none on tape or disk. Neither were there any state-paid readers as there are today; we depended entirely on student volunteers.

The special teacher for blind students was Mrs. Mallard, 4' 10", 190 pounds. The students said she waddled when she walked. They referred to her as Ducky. She had a maddening habit of not informing us when she left the room, with the result that our questions were often greeted with silence.

The only class I truly enjoyed was French. The grammars were in Braille, and there was virtually no work on the board. Besides, I loved its sound, its precision, and the way it felt in my mouth.

The instructor, Miss Haflin, was a tyrant. If you weren't ready when she called on you, you would be pierced with, "Sorry I woke you. Go back to sleep." She moved the class along swiftly, making us memorize La Fontaine fables and folksongs and use their vocabularies in written sentences and class conversation.

Toward the end of the term, she drew me aside.

"When you finish this," she said, "you can skip French Two." And I did.

But the fun in French made hardly a dent in my otherwise disquieting feelings in these school years. No longer was I the center of attention, the pampered darling whom Miss Guy bounced up and down singing, "Rosy, Posy, Puddin' 'n' Pie." My roommates had their own studies and problems. Chip was working toward a Cornell scholarship (which she ultimately received), and Pill was planning to do secretarial work, feeling confident that she would land a job (which she did, as a dictaphone typist in a downtown office). There was no reason to practice the piano—an hour a week was enough to keep up with Miss Keybler's assignments. And now, in my teens, I realized how blindness hurt the most: not getting dates with boys. Eyes were the way you made friends. You had to be able to return a glance. Papa said, "It's good Rose can't see—she'd be a devil with the boys."

Once Jean and a boyfriend invited me to go with them to the Roseland Ballroom, a public dance hall on West Fifty-seventh Street. The music had that big band sound, and I was thoroughly enjoying myself until Roy, in the middle of a waltz, said, "Hey, you're a good dancer; good-lookin', too. You know, if you could see, I'd marry you."

I thought, "You presumptuous ass," and snapped, "What makes you think I'd have you?" I never wanted to go out with them again.

Other girls had someone to go out with, dress up for, talk about to other girls. Not I. I tried in vain to ignore the loneliness, resentment and the inferiority I felt as I watched my sisters primp for Saturday dates. Would it always be this way, I wondered? Would I always feel an outsider? Did this mean I wasn't appealing to men? It was something I couldn't talk about to anyone—it was embarrassing, and anyway it wouldn't do any good. People seemed to take it for granted that if you couldn't see, you couldn't feel—at least not sexually.

The closest I'll ever come to a love experience, I thought bitterly, is as Oliva (a role I played in "Water Upon Fire," a one-act play we were doing at the time), and opposite a girl taking a male part, at that!

There was no way of meeting boys, not even blind boys. Coeducational activities were taboo at the Lighthouse. The directors feared that dating might result in the spawning of blind babies. The danger of this unnatural separation became apparent when two teenage girls were discovered necking with each other on the stairs between the fifth floor and the roof of the Lighthouse. Like Mimi, they were immediately expelled.

As usual, however, Miss Guy was not oblivious to the desires of her growing girls. She invited a group of YMCA men to monthly dances in the auditorium we knew so well. Anticipation of each dance was feverish. I would go home to Brooklyn Friday night to get my blackheads squeezed, eyebrows tweezed, hair set, dress and jewelry borrowed. On the big night Jean would deck me out, put on my makeup—complete with mascara, eye shadow, rouge, and powder—and arrange every strand of hair, instructing me to check it each hour.

"Don't expect it to stay this way all night," she admonished. "You have to keep brushing it to make it stay fresh and shiny. And if you eat anything, you'll need more lipstick."

At the dance I threaded my way through the crowd to find my pals. The hubbub of introductions, the music, the rustle of silk dresses, and the perfume in the air made an electric excitement around us. With the first sounds of the orchestra came the magic moment: "May I have this dance?"

More often than not, he was a lemon—he had halitosis, or B.O., or couldn't dance or couldn't talk. Oh God, I thought, if only he had a sense of rhythm I think I could stand it. He could keep doing the same steps all night if only he did them in time. But perhaps the next partner would be better. If he asked again, I hoped I would find the courage to say, "No, thank you, I'm a bit tired right now."

The first one sat me down between two strange men in one of the rows of chairs that lined the wall. No sooner had the band struck up again when the man on my right leaned over. Taking my hand and drawing me to my feet, he asked, "Shall we?"

Before I could answer, we were sailing—this one, although equally taciturn, danced well. He was easy to follow, held me in a kind of pleasing vise. I was glad when he came back for more dances.

The men themselves were courteous, but dull and impersonal. The girls who went home with dates were some of the pretty, sighted secretaries who often attended. There were some exceptions—Chip was asked out once or twice. But somehow not being singled out for their private attentions never bothered me. It was enough to whirl around the floor with the three or four men who danced well. At most dances, whether it was waltzes, fox trots, Paul Jones, broom dances, or elimination contests, I had a good time, sitting out only for ice cream and cake.

Watching us on the dance floor, Miss Guy had a revolutionary idea. To make us more agile and graceful, she engaged Marjorie Forsheimer, a Columbia graduate in physical education, to teach us classical dance. The idea that blind girls could learn to dance was unheard-of in those days and would probably surprise many people today. Since a number of us were at the Lighthouse Saturday afternoons for drama rehearsals, she arranged for us to have an early snack and scheduled the dance classes for seven o'clock the same evening.

Marjorie began by asking us to take hands in a large circle and walk right, left, forward, and back. She then had us drop hands, take two steps back, and repeat the sequence independently. This was a challenge, for you had to judge kinesthetically the distance between yourself and the person in front of you and keep that distance the same as you progressed, as well as remember the size of the circle. Some of us toed in, some out. Some walked flatfooted; some heads were out of alignment. I was so stiff and painfully self-conscious that I actually cried.

"Swing your arms. Let yourselves go. There's not a thing to bump into—if you step on someone that means she is not taking large enough steps." With practice eventually we moved with freedom and confidence.

In the second lesson Marjorie asked us to move to the opposite end of the room. Clapping her hands, she called to us one at a time to walk, run, then leap toward her.

"Higher, higher," she would insist in our leaps. "Straighten that back leg."

We danced barefoot in flowing cheesecloth costumes to the accompaniment of tarantellas, Brahms and Schubert waltzes, and Kreisler's "Liebesfreud." Marjorie stressed relaxation. We were rag dolls with heavy floppy arms and legs; we were trees whose branches moved at the will of the wind.

She showed us how to pantomime greeting, farewell, anger, sadness, disappointment, and joy. We then tried to incorporate them in situations. To Chopin's A Major Prelude, Marjorie asked us to pantomime the burial of a bird. "Not so far apart with your hands. Your bird isn't that big," she corrected as we began. So we stooped over, ready to place him in the earth.

"No, you can't just put him down. You'll have to look around for the best spot, where there's some shelter. Turn your head right, left—now walk about, look here, there—now you see a good place. It's grassy and the earth is soft enough. Let's kneel and try out the earth all around it. Now spread the earth apart. That's it! Now, very gently, place him in, and cover him up."

Whereas Majorie's main interest was freedom and expression, our next teacher, Miss Hally, drilled us in technique. Using chairs as bars, we spent the first half-hour bending, stretching, kicking, balancing, developing every muscle in our bodies. When, at the next lesson, we groaned about paralysis and aching muscles suffered for days after class, she said, "Fine, that shows how much you need it. Take a hot bath and do the same exercises over again."

In the second half-hour we learned ballet positions, steps, and dances, eventually graduating to blocked slippers and simple routines on point.

All of us had crushes on her successor, Henrietta Peterson. Unlike Hally or Marjorie, she was always remote, tantalizingly impersonal. We felt that she, more than any of our teachers, personified dance: Tall and willowy, she moved effortlessly, her feet seeming scarcely to touch the ground.

Our heartthrob always arrived in riding togs, accompanied by a gentleman who sat patiently and waited for her throughout every lesson. We could tell by her Quelques Fleurs perfume the moment she floated into the auditorium. To demonstrate technique and position, she let us touch her legs, hands, arms, torso, shoulders, back, and head. We marveled at her form and grace. Sometimes she placed our hands or legs in the correct position for an arabesque or pirouette. She taught us how to do turns and how to fall with relaxation. The trick was to bend your knees and fall forward with your hands extended in front of you. If you could relax, you felt no pain and got no bruises.

Mrs. Peterson took us still further into the discipline of ballet. Week after week we worked on *pas de chats*, *tour jetés*, backbends, high kicks, and quick turns, circling the whole room. In time she considered us ready for interpretation. We danced Narcissus playing with his reflection in the water; Bacchus gathering, crushing, and devouring grapes, whirling, stamping, staggering until we fell limp to the floor. We played witches, tracing magic circles in moonlit glades with spangled scarves, casting spells that killed the heroine; shepherds who turned into princes and awakened sleeping beauties with a kiss.

By now we were dancing for Lighthouse exhibitions at the Commodore Hotel in billowy, leaf-shaped muslin skirts, tight bodices, pink tights, and satin slippers.

For me, those dance sessions were pure ecstasy—a release from the strictures of everyday life. I never tired. The longer I danced, the more I wanted to. Floating, whirling, leaping, flying around that room, I felt it was good to be alive.

But those dance classes meant far more to all of us than the mere temporary release of pent-up energy or even the increase in our vocabulary of movement. They improved our coordination, balance, flexibility, sense of direction, muscle control, and capacity for relaxation. Years later I stepped off a streetcar and was instantly knocked down by a closely passing automobile. I simply picked myself up and continued on my way without a bruise. I'm certain it was all that teenage body discipline and practice in falling relaxed that saved me.

However, except for the dances and dance lessons, I look back on my high school days as a kind of Dark Ages. Nothing at school had any relevance for me. Everything about it—the teachers, the classwork, the other students—all seemed remote. Part of it, I think, was boarding with older people, being away from home and not having anyone who cared—or so it seemed. I am sure, too, that part of it was trying to find some identity in the maelstrom of five thousand students. It was as though I were in some shadowy world, half-awake, going through programmed routines. I felt adrift, lost, terribly alone most of the time. This wasn't such a safe world, after all. You could have a glorious childhood—friends, a running streak of luck—and then be left to go it alone.

From the beginning of my senior year I felt a gnawing concern about the future. Before the introduction of counseling services, students had only their leanings or grade indications as a guide to a career. All my friends were going on to college. Knowing what a desert high school had been, I sought advice from one of the teachers. She merely referred me to a Mrs. Mallard, who was equally blank.

Certainly no one in the family could advise me. The expectation was that once you got through high school—which in our family was a privilege—you were supposed to get out and work. But for what job was I qualified? Because I was home only on weekends, they thought of me as being already on my own.

Papa was still eking out a living and making the family miserable. Becky was a year behind me at Brooklyn High School. Jean was working at manicuring and loathing every minute of it. Sarah was helping Papa in the shop.

None of us had anything in common. Already we were beginning to go our separate ways. My piano had been the first step away from them. Then came books and dramatics and all those Lighthouse people in whose world I felt so much more at home than in my family's. Yet there were always the blood tie—the scenes and situations we had shared and which made an instinctive bond.

If I didn't go to college, what would I do? It might mean staying home and doing nothing, and that would be worse than death. If I did go to college, and my grades were good enough, perhaps I could teach. I had read from time to time about blind people who had succeeded in obtaining appointments in spite of prejudice, and who had taught in regular classes. Somehow it was a challenge I wanted to meet.

To my family, graduation was like a birthday—or having your tonsils out—a little unusual, but nothing to fuss over. None of them attended. To the accompaniment of "Pomp and Circumstance," played by the school orchestra, I walked with one of my classmates down the aisle and up the steps of the platform to receive my diploma. In her full resonant voice, Dean MacVeigh gave a stirring farewell message:

"You have all your lives before you. Always remember that it doesn't matter so much what hardships life brings you. What counts is how you react to them."

With these words ringing in my ears, and an intense loneliness lurking within me, I went home to Brooklyn—definitely decided on college.

[6]

My New Music Teacher

For the most part, Hunter differed little from high school. All classes took place in the same building, and again I was just one of thousands of students. Now, however, there was no special teacher to print material into Braille or vice versa. Quizzes and term papers had to be typed. One twenty-page paper, done at home on an old Corona portable, came out entirely blank—the ribbon had failed to inform me that it wasn't working that day. My only exchange with students was over a hastily gulped cup of coffee or lunch in the locker-filled basement. One always had to fly over notes before a quiz, tackle in ten minutes an assignment that required an hour, or get a book out of the library. Besides, I didn't have the time, initiative, or confidence to join any of the clubs.

I went on with French and registered uneventfully for composition, German, trigonometry, Latin, and science, but when I appeared for the required physical education course, I was flatly denied admission.

The reason?

"The course is strenuous and possibly dangerous for you."

I was appalled. I explained that I had had five years of dance—that I swam, rode horseback, and skated.

"What kind of dance?"

"Mainly interpretive and ballet."

"How could you learn ballet?"

"The teacher merely described what she was doing and demonstrated by touch."

I begged to be given at least a trial, but it was only after my agreement to sign a waiver releasing the college from all responsibility that I was allowed to take the courses. All that for a class in calisthenics, marching, and folk dancing! I could only hope that the next blind applicant would be automatically admitted like any other student.

One of the best things I found at Hunter was Esther Sweedler. We met the first day and have been friends ever since. The students described her as stunning, as having "a model's figure," dark eyes, jet-black hair, oval face, and perfect features. She shared with me lunches, party dresses, and occasionally one of her boyfriends. We hitchhiked to Niagara Falls one time, on five dollars apiece, and to Washington for a similar sum. We spent two weeks at Camp Louise in the Blue Ridge Mountains one summer and audited courses at the University of Michigan another.

Esther lived on the sixth floor of an East Ninety-ninth Street tenement with an asthmatic mother, two sisters, and a brother. Mrs. Sweedler, the sole support of the family, worked as janitress until Esther, just before her senior year, dropped out of college to take a job at Macy's. A year later she returned, and along with her B.A. degree, picked up a Phi Beta Kappa key. She went on to take a master's degree in mathematics at Columbia and then a teaching job on Staten Island.

She was always involved with three or four men at one time. Once, after a rare two-day absence from college, she came back with a black eye and bruises on her forehead. A man had attacked her on the way home. All of us were intrigued by the way she saved herself.

"I was lucky. It was raining and I used my umbrella on him. He tried to drag me into a doorway and I said, 'Let go of me, I'm menstruating—and he dropped me pronto.'"

One day halfway through my freshman year, I was dreaming away at the piano in one of the Lighthouse music rooms when Miss Guy popped in with a visitor.

"Excuse us, Posy, I'd like you to meet Mr. Munger. I'm giving him a tour of the Lighthouse, and he's interested in our young people. Would you mind playing something for him?"

My reaction was anything but gracious. I hated being put on exhibit. At school there always had been visitors who "would just love to hear you read," and at the Lighthouse one of us was always being called upon to play, sing, recite, dance, or perform some caper or other to interest or instruct people. But here was a Lighthouse contributor; I had no choice. Still, I was not going to show off. I chose the very simple "To a Wild Rose" by MacDowell.

When I had finished, Mr. Munger said, "Thank you. You gave me much pleasure."

Two weeks later Miss Guy informed me that he had awarded me a four-year scholarship to the Manhattan School of Music.

"Ye gods!" I said. "After that little piece! I don't think I deserve it."

Actually, I had mixed feelings about the scholarship. It was an opportunity to move ahead with my music, but how ironic for it to come now when I was deluged with work! Surely I would have to prove worthy of it. And when would I find the time to practice?

The school director awed me with the achievements of my new music teacher. He had given concerts throughout the United States and Europe, had played with the major orchestras, had accompanied Richard Crooks and Caruso, and was currently broadcasting weekly a two-piano series with famous Marlowe Lane on the N.B.C. network. I was definitely not ready for this man.

But late one afternoon I met the great Rudolph Gruen. His voice, manner, and movement gave me the impression of a self-conscious person, dog-tired after a full day of teaching, uncomfortable at the prospect of a blind student. I wanted to slink off and forget the lessons. He asked me to play three pieces and made no comment until at the end of the third he said in a cold, flat voice, "You play musically, but not always exactly what the composer wrote. And you've acquired some

My New Music Teacher

bad habits in hand position. How do you study your music?"

I explained that most classics could be borrowed from the Braille Division of the New York Public Library and that volunteers were available to transcribe the more modern pieces into Braille.

When I left Mr. Gruen's studio that day, I knew he had reservations about his new student. It was depressing, as always, to find someone uncertain of your ability because of your blindness. In all fairness, however, part of his reaction might stem from a quandary about the method of teaching me. I determined that if he were too shy to bring it out in the open at my first lesson, I would.

Next time, with him seated at the piano trying to explain correct hand position, and me standing next to him, I seized the opportunity to show him how I could better understand.

"I can follow you better," I ventured, "if you let me put my hand over yours." From then on, both of us were more at ease. He let me touch his arms and hands as he sat at the keyboard.

He made me begin all over again with hand-position drills and finger-strengthening exercises. Undoing bad habits was, of course, twice as hard as learning the right way from the start. It was monotonous and frustrating. I had never learned that each finger must be able to move up and down independently, that the knuckles must form an arch to balance and support the weight of the arm on the fingertips. No one had ever taught me how to develop strong fingers and hands or how to relax wrists and arms—indispensable preliminaries to confident, powerful playing. This is happening much too late, I thought, I'll never catch up.

He was meticulous in his corrections, insisting on the perfection of every detail in notation, dynamics, phrasing, and pedaling. For the first time I learned that the down and up movements of the wrist indicate the beginning and end of phrases, and that the advanced movement of the thumb is imperative for smoothness and speed in scales and arpeggios. As I progressed through Czerny and Clementi to Bach inventions and fugues, Beethoven sonatas, and Chopin études, I realized that my new teacher was giving me a foundation applicable to any composition I would ever attempt.

His manner, however, continued cold and austere. Not until I heard him play in public did I perceive the man's inner fire. He invited another student and me to his concert at Town Hall. As he walked on, my friend leaned over and whispered "Medium height, painfully thin, angular, cadaverous face, sparse hair—but sensitive eyes."

He opened with his own arrangement of a Bach Sicilienne and followed with the dramatic F Minor Sonata by Brahms. His power, speed, leaps, and variety of tone color had me on the edge of my seat. Would my playing ever approach anything like that? Before the next lesson, I told him how much I had enjoyed the concert and the two-piano Sunday broadcasts.

"I must tell you a wonderful joke about that," he said. "Did you happen to hear the Rachmaninoff 'Paques'?"

"The piece that simulates Easter bells? Yes, very effective."

"Well, it brought quite a bit of mail. We posted one

card on the bulletin board. It said, 'Why the hell don't you do your practicing at home?'"

Rudy, as I came to know him, was an eccentric genius. In addition to a full schedule of teaching, concert-giving, and broadcasting, he read omnivorously, carried on a wide correspondence, and still found time for his first love, composition. He rose early each morning and ran a mile in Central Park before breakfast. He was compulsively punctual, noting in his datebook "1:59" for a two o'clock appointment. Mountain climbing fascinated him. As a young man he had climbed extensively in the Alps, Rockies, and Adirondacks. He had a natural inner calm, nourished perhaps by attraction to the great Eastern religions. He followed many of their practices: exercise to tone the body, meditation, and—in time—fasting. Today thousands of people meditate to find peace and increase self-understanding, awareness, and inspiration, but in those days people regarded such habits as bizarre.

Most of the time we were lost in the music. But eventually—I thought it would never happen—he paused for a bit of conversation.

At the time, he was deeply involved in the study of Science of Mind and wondered if it might help restore my sight. His religious strain came as no surprise—an older sister was a missionary in China; his uncle was a Lutheran minister. But I was annoyed that he was still grappling with the blind business and amazed that anyone as rational as he could believe that, merely by affirming it, I'd be able to see. I explained that I had recently been to a distinguished ophthalmologist and that he had declared: "Rose, I think you'd better get your fun in other ways." Translated, that meant that the scars were of long duration and therefore impossible to remove.

Rudy's reply took me by surprise.

"Of course I never think of you as not being able to see. You're sure you're not fooling us all?"

He couldn't have said a nicer thing, for when other people forgot, I did, too.

At other lessons, he stopped to rhapsodize about his new ideas on health.

"I met a marvelous man the other day," he said, "seventy-five years old, but looks forty. He claims the three killers in America are white bread, white sugar, and carbonated drinks. I've been plagued with fatigue, just a dreadful exhausted feeling all the time. I'm sure it's the junk I've been eating—cake, candy, potato chips, things like that. Now when I crave something sweet, I get dates, figs, or fresh fruit and make a whole meal of salad. I'm beginning to feel alive again."

Soon he was warning me against combining meat with potatoes, sugars with starch. When, at seventeen, you are studying with a renowned pianist, you are likely to do anything he suggests. Soon Mother began fixing carrot-and-onion mixtures. Nothing but rough, dark bread came into the house, and sugar was eliminated from tea and coffee.

At home over an Easter vacation in 1933, I found that Papa had decided to retire, reducing his support of the family from little to nothing. The family would no longer be able to send me five dollars a week for expenses. I would now be obliged to earn at least that much for my room and board in Manhattan.

I applied to Emil Meinke, the new Lighthouse director, himself blind, for parttime work in the music department. He hired me to teach after school Tuesdays and Thursdays, and on Saturday mornings—salary, ten dollars a week.

My forty students ranged in age from six to sixty. They varied in degrees of blindness and retardation; most of them smelled as though they had been sewn into their underwear for months. They seemed to be taking piano lessons only because they were free.

Every lesson was anathema. The children stumbled around the keyboard week after week, making the same mistakes. Because of their dulled senses of touch, the adults found Braille music difficult if not impossible. I discovered that there was no fun in teaching music, or probably anything for that matter, unless the pupil was gifted or really wanted to learn.

The pay was insulting even for a beginning teacher, but who could argue with Meinke? He was arrogant and ruthless—"sadistic," the staff called him. Hardly had he assumed his position at the Lighthouse when he began to fire people, apparently to show he was boss. He barked orders at employees and made sexual advances to female members of the staff while his wife, whom he had made head of the music department, taught in another part of the building.

How could anything so sinister happen to an agency which had begun so idealistically! Those of us who had come there as children knew what a Lighthouse could be. We were heartbroken at the way Meinke treated Alma Guy. He had terminated her administrative responsibilities in the recreation department and undermined her relationship with the staff. Indeed, the illness which led to her death began during his régime.

I avoided any contact with him. I was mortally afraid of the man. One Saturday morning Sarah rode in with me for my nine o'clock pupil. We arrived at the Lighthouse two minutes late. Rather than incur his anger, we about-faced and took the subway home.

For weeks I tried to gather enough courage to ask for a raise. Finally I stopped in his office and timidly uttered the request.

He picked up the phone and snapped to the switchboard operator, "Get me the bookkeeper."

Then, "Put five dollars more in Resnick's envelope."

Under Meinke's administration the Lighthouse changed from a free and friendly place to an institution. He was intent on putting everything on a "business" basis. People were no longer Bill, Mary, John—individuals with identity, with worth as such—they were cases with numbers. The more numbers he could show, the better. Shortly after he assumed his job, it was evident that in addition to putting the Lighthouse on a "paying" basis, he himself was growing affluent. His weekends were stretching into four and five days, and there was talk of a flourishing enterprise, a New England resort, run by the Meinkes. When someone tipped him off that the board of directors was about to fire him for embezzlement of funds, Meinke shot himself.

It was my first observation of irresponsibility and lack of integrity on the part of an agency executive, and it was painful.

The affair was hushed up because the board feared public criticism of its failure to properly manage agency finances. The clients felt that if the board had been aware of the drastic changes taking place, Meinke could never have succeeded in destroying the dynamic programs pioneered by Guy.

* * *

My New Music Teacher

By the time my senior year rolled around, I knew exactly where I was headed: I would teach French. I had had three years of it in high school and four in college, with straight *A*'s. My instructor had turned the class over to me from time to time, and maintaining the students' attention proved no problem for me. If we needed help in vocabulary, as we did quite often, one of the good students would look it up in the always-handy Larousse.

But a worse snag lay ahead.

In addition to the B.A. degree, New York State required teaching candidates to pass Regents examinations. When I applied to take them, I was informed that blind people were barred from teaching and hence not eligible to take the examinations.* It was a brutal disappointment. I realized that it might be hard to find a college president willing to give me a chance. Others had been lucky, and I thought I might be, too. It had never occurred to me to question my right to take an examination open to other students. Yet, remembering the resistance I had encountered when registering for gym class, I should have foreseen such an eventuality. I felt humiliated, inferior in the eyes of the teachers and students. Inasmuch as Hunter was a teacher-training institution, I wondered why the administration or faculty hadn't discussed my objective with me. Perhaps that old pessimist at high school who had disparaged the idea of

---

* In 1967, the New York legislature amended the Education Law to read, "No regulations established by the Commissioner or by the School District, shall prohibit, prevent or disqualify any person, who is otherwise qualified, from competing, participating, and registering for examination, or from obtaining a teacher's certificate or from qualifying for a position as a teacher solely by reason of his or her blindness."

my going to college was right. Perhaps I had wasted four years. I had proved to myself that I could do it, and now I was a college graduate. So what?

It all seemed so unreasonable, so unjust. And as always, there was no one to talk it over with. Esther was out of college that year and deep in myriad romances. Rudy was off on a tour, then to the Adirondacks for the summer. What would I do now? Another blank wall!

Graduation held none of the glamour, excitement, or sense of achievement for me that it did for my college classmates. I invited no one to the exercises. Not one member of my family was present. Instead of satisfaction at the realization of a goal I had set for myself, graduation was an anticlimax. The props had been pulled out from under me. There was no longer anything to work toward. Fate was having a laugh at my expense. What was this life all about, anyhow? "These are the most wonderful years of your lives," the main speaker had declared. I thought, "God forbid!"

[7]

Fontainebleau

A FEW MONTHS before graduation, Esther and I wandered into a Lexington Avenue teashop famous for its fortune-teller.

"I see you seated at a grand piano," she told me, stirring the tea leaves, "with a lot of people listening. You're going to take a trip for sure."

"I'm afraid all my trips will be on the subway between Brooklyn and Manhattan," I said and dismissed the incident as a joke.

Not long after that, Margaret Tucker, a New York society woman who was interested in the Lighthouse Players and who read for me each week, invited me to a cocktail party at her house. "It's to welcome my friend Polly Damrosch back from Europe. You know, the daughter of the New York Symphony conductor."

I said I'd be delighted.

"Will you mind if they ask you to play?"

"Golly, I never get enough time to practice," I said, "but I should be able to do a piece or two."

I was relieved that Walter Damrosch himself was not present at the party. Margaret's other guests were unpretentious, relaxed people, and I felt entirely at ease. They not only wanted "a bit of music," but of all things, asked me to improvise. I explained that I had never done that for an audience but that I would try. I asked them to give me four notes to use as a theme and, as I had often done at home, played around with it, first as a march, then in waltz time. They seemed appreciative but not wildly enthusiastic.

Early next morning Margaret was on the phone. "How would you like to study in Europe next summer?"

"What!"

"Those people you played for yesterday were Mr. Damrosch's Scholarship Committee. They want you to have one."

"Not me! I can't believe it!" It was unreal.

"It's true," she said. "You'll be studying piano and composition at the Fontainebleau Conservatory of Music. I'm thrilled for you. You'll be sailing on the *Rochambeau* early in July. The session is three months. Let me know if I can help with shots or anything."

I don't remember saying goodbye. I dashed up to my room, jumped up and down on the bed, then raced around the halls looking for someone to tell the exciting news. In a state of disbelief, I shopped, was vaccinated, collected a passport, and packed a standup steamertrunk. The farewells went smoothly until I came to my sister Jean. Then both of us burst into tears.

I was one of sixty students awarded scholarships that

summer. The girl with whom I shared a cabin on the *Rochambeau* accompanied me on walks around the decks and to meals. As luck would have it, the night I actually sat "at a grand piano with lots of people listening" was the only night the sea was rough. The ship rolled and bucked giant waves, and I chased middle C up and down the keyboard, wondering how the waiters had managed to serve dinner. To take all our minds off the situation, I played half the planned program, then switched to community singing.

The Conservatory of Fontainebleau, some forty miles outside Paris, occupied three buildings: the palace, where the students lived; the music building next door; and the refectory, where faculty and students had their meals. Jerry Reynolds, coordinator of student activities, registered us and assigned our rooms. Realizing that I would need help in getting about the campus and to meals, Margaret had arranged for someone to share mine.

"Mme. Rozan will share your room," Jerry informed me. "She's a spry seventy-eight, but she'll be very helpful. You'll have a good chance to practice speaking French because she knows not one word of English."

I was delighted at the prospect of improving my French, but why had they selected a lady of that vintage to room with a girl of twenty-one? Wouldn't such an arrangement tend to separate me from the other students? I admitted to myself that I did need the help, but I was disappointed that it couldn't have been from another student.

As Madame and I crossed the cobblestoned courtyard of the palace, I noticed that she was a heavy woman, shorter than I, and had a gravelly voice. Obviously she had never walked with a blind person before: She clutched my arm with the grip of a longshoreman, hoisting me up the three flights of marble steps en route to our room on the top floor. My guardian acted as though she thought I was going to break at any minute.

"*Prenez garde, prenez garde,*" she kept warning me, when there was nothing to be careful about. I explained that if she paused briefly at the beginning of each flight, I could manage easily. But for days her fear persisted.

Our room was huge and plain: two dressers, two beds, and two chairs, as I recall. I unlocked my trunk and began unpacking at once. As I laid things on the bed or dresser, Madame Rozan picked them up and put them where she thought they ought to go. I tried gently to tell her that unless I put them away myself I wouldn't know where to find them.

"But I will find them for you. This is my duty," she said.

It was no use. This lady had a mind of her own. That night, when stentorian snores assured me she was asleep, I got up and rearranged things in the drawers, in the closet, and on the bathroom shelf.

Jerry had announced that we must post on the bulletin board the day and hour we wished to take a bath. The only tub in the building was on the top floor, and the price was fifteen cents.

At meals, Mme. Rozan buttered my bread, cut my meat, and washed the dusty fruit served for dessert. She did everything but chew the food for me. I found myself submitting, rather than protesting. Rarely did the students include me in conversation, and I did nothing about that either. For some reason I kept silent. I felt miserably left-out and alone. I hated myself for my apparent inability to bridge the gap. I thought bitterly, "That's the worst part of being blind; people treat you as though you were different, an outsider." I wanted so much to be a part of their fun and fellowship. Was it my dependence on Mme. Rozan and our being together so much of the time that separated me from them? Hearing them talk about their exciting dates in Paris intensified my feelings of isolation and inferiority. I tried to remind myself that I was there to improve my piano-playing, not for romance. To add to my misery, I came down with a full-blown case of hives. Most nights that week I cried myself to sleep.

I finally found a way to get to Paris. I had brought with me from New York a letter of introduction to an American who lived there. Why not have Mme. Rozan put me on the train and write Mrs. Clark, asking if she would meet me at the station and show me at least a little of the city? My letter brought no reply, but I decided I would take the plunge—I would chance it alone. From the Paris depot I could taxi to the tour bus and return the same way. Mme. Rozan must be allowed to think that someone would meet me at the Paris station, or else she would never let me make the trip.

She accompanied me to the train, bought a second-class ticket, and looked around for someone to help me debark in Paris. She stopped an exceedingly tall girl and asked what class she would be sitting in.

"*Première*," she said. "*Pourquoi?*"

Madame asked if she would see that I got off safely in Paris.

"*Mais certainement,*" she said as we climbed aboard.

"That's very kind of you," I said in English, recognizing an American.

"Thank God," the girl said, with a lusty laugh I was to find characteristic. "I was just coming to the end of my French. I'm Conway Sawyer. I'm quite free this afternoon, so I'll see you later," she said as we parted for our respective seats.

I was in rare luck, for it was Conway who showed me whatever I saw of Paris that summer. We began at an outdoor café. Over a cognac for her, an apricot parfait for me, she described the broad avenues, the trees, the gesticulating ladies passing by, the public urinals, the notorious, chaotic traffic.

"A concierge told me," she said, "that in case of accident, the pedestrian is guilty; he pays the fine."

Conway was a completely uninhibited person, quick, witty, and obviously generous.

"What are you doing here?" I asked. "Tell me about yourself."

By coincidence, she lived on Park Avenue, around the corner from the Lighthouse. Her father, a well-known architect, had designed and built their house. Her mother was an accomplished pianist who knew everybody who was anybody and entertained lavishly. Conway had played on Broadway for five years, but finding that her height limited her roles, left the stage for a more satisfying career in sculpture. She had studied with Archipenko and was now enrolled at the Beaux Arts School in Fontainebleau.

"I can't stand it much longer," she said. "I plan to quit soon. It's terribly conservative. No point in staying. Can you get away again some time? While I'm here, I'll be glad to do a little of this town with you."

We spent the rest of that afternoon at the Louvre. Ignoring the Do Not Touch signs, I proceeded to Braille

Fontainebleau

the Michelangelo slaves when an indignant guard rushed over to protest. As soon as Conway explained the circumstances, however, he apologized and even followed us around, bringing a bench for me to stand on when figures were beyond my reach.

My new friend's knowledge of art greatly enriched my appreciation of what we were seeing; her comments about line, proportion, unity, and contrast helped me integrate into a meaningful whole what by touch I could discern only as separate elements.

Next we moved onto a wing of paintings. When Conway talked about clouds or mountains or figures "in the distance," I remembered what Prof and Major Bill had taught us about perspective. Where the artist had used a palette knife or other cutting tool, I could trace the designs with my fingers. Their parallels in music helped me understand the differences in style between baroque, classical, and impressionistic paintings.

"This place takes a lifetime to see," Conway said, "but you've had a tiny introduction. That's about as much as anyone can absorb at one time, anyway."

It was twenty years before I got back to the Louvre but no visit was as vivid as that first one with Conway. In the short time she remained at Fontainebleau, we took a walk along the Seine, attended a service at Notre Dame Cathedral, and visited the Valentin Hauy Braille Music Library. Conway bought me volumes of Bach, Haydn, Beethoven, and Debussy—the first music I ever owned.

From the music building, at any hour of the day, you could hear students exercising their vocal chords, drilling on pianos and violins, or blowing horns. We practiced in small, hot, low-ceilinged rooms which the concierge tried vainly to cool by hosing down the floors daily. Jerry assigned me to a no-nonsense instructor who tore me to pieces at every lesson. I had the feeling she wondered what in the world I was doing there with all those advanced students.

Once a week, each of us had to play for the *grand maître,* eighty-year-old M. Philipp. His name was familiar to most of us from his Spartan exercises. Instead of a forbidding pedagogue, however, we found a genial listener. When I finished playing a piece, he'd put his arm around me and murmur, *"Très bien, mon enfant. Continuez à travailler."*

The most extraordinary member of the Fontainebleau faculty was the famous teacher of harmony and composition, Mlle. Nadia Boulanger. A pupil of Fauré, she had known Debussy, was a close friend of Stravinsky, and had taught Aaron Copland, Roy Harris, Robert Russell Bennett, and many other well-known composers. Long before the public accepted Stravinsky, Bartok, Hindemith, and Schoenberg, she recognized their genius and imparted it to her students. "Rules," she said, "serve only as gymnastics, as discipline. Once mastered, they can and should be ignored."

From the moment I met Nadia Boulanger I felt the impact of a robust personality. It was at the foot of the stairs in the music building. She grasped my hand and said in a vibrant husky voice, "You're Rose Resnick. I know all about you. Polly Damrosch told me about you in Vienna. Come along."

Whereupon she placed my hand on the banister and preceded me up the stairs into her studio and to the piano.

"Do you have absolute pitch?" she asked.

"I think so but I'm not sure."

She struck a note.

"What is ziss?"

"It sounds like D."

"It sounds like, and it is, and you have. Now I'm going to play a piece, and I want you to tell me which key I'm in each time it modulates."

She then flew into Bach's C-sharp Major Prelude.

"Oh," I gasped, "those sharp keys may mix me up."

"All right. I transpose."

She immediately moved the Prelude, a rapid, frequently modulating piece, into the key of C. I named each change of key as I heard it.

"You're fine," was her verdict. "You will find someone in class to write out your compositions. That shy lad, Andy, from the University of Michigan—I'll ask him to do it. We will start with two-part counterpoint, then a fugue, then a string quartet."

I cringed at her expectations.

Andy began by walking me to my room after class, then leaving chocolate, wine, apples, and perfume at my door, and finally inviting me to poetry readings and rides in an open horse-drawn carriage in the Bois. The poetry turned into wrestling matches to keep my clothes on. He apologized for the first intimate kiss, saying, "You're so nice. I hate to do this to you."

"Don't be insulting," I said, wanting to be treated like any other girl, and rather enjoying the final intimations of a bit of romance. Andy helped make the summer a liberal education in more than music.

Boulanger's work day began at 8:00 A.M. and continued without a stop until 5:00. Bread and bananas, snatched periodically out of a lower desk-drawer, served as breakfast and lunch. In class, the air crackled with her vitality. She would hand out the scores of Josquin Des Prez, Debussy's "Le Martyre de Saint Sébastian," and Stravinsky's "Les Noces," and ask the class to sing the parts at sight and analyze the form.

One day she called on some of us for appraisals of various composers. She asked Andy what he thought of opera.

"I agree with Debussy," he said. "In opera they sing too much."

The class roared. Then she pounced on me.

"Rose Resnick, what do you think of Strauss?"

"His orchestrations sometimes get a bit noisy," I said, feeling very stupid.

"That's when he's best," declared Boulanger categorically.

One brave student asked her which she considered the greatest piece ever written.

"The Mozart Clarinet Quintet," she said, without a moment's hesitation.

The Fontainebleau diploma certified that students who had completed the work in basic composition and piano were qualified to teach. Mme. Rozan treated the document as though it were the medal of the Legion of Honor. She guarded it so carefully that when the time came to leave, neither of us could find it.

On the boat going home I wondered how Rudy would rate my progress and what the experience would mean for my future. I had written my deep gratitude to Margaret Tucker, but I realized she had slipped out of the

Fontainebleau

lives of us Lighthouse girls forever—she was now the wife of John Saltonstall, the senator from Massachusetts. The diploma would look good on my résumés, but how it would affect my career I was not certain.

[8]

Début

Back in Brooklyn I found a handsome addition to the family, a cuddly nephew. My sister Sarah had decided she could do better without her husband, so she and little Julian moved back home.

Becky was working hard as a secretary and at getting married. Jean had married and unmarried a Pole and was still slaving away at manicuring. I resumed the long dreary rides on the subway to long dreary hours of teaching at the Lighthouse.

But Fontainebleau had refueled my interest in practice and Rudy was quick to notice it. "I think you ought to play a program for your family and friends," he said, at the end of an especially good lesson.

"Heavens, do you think I'm ready?"

"No one ever feels ready. It will be a good experience for you."

Début

So, in one of the large rooms of the Manhattan School, I played my first recital. Only Rudy knew how nervous I was, waiting in the wings to go on. My hands were ice—I was sure not a muscle would move. Strange things quivered in the region of my stomach.

"All artists get queasy before a concert," Rudy comforted me.

Once past the first few minutes, the butterflies subsided. Rudy was backstage waiting for me during intermission.

"You're doing beautifully," he said, in his characteristically quiet way.

"I wasn't conscious the whole time," I confessed. "Just sort of floated off in space."

"That's when you play best. When you know a piece well, have practiced it slowly and love it, it becomes a part of you and you can trust your subconscious to take over."

By the end of the concert I wanted to go on playing all night. Rudy was relaxed, smiling, unusually animated. He had brought along the other half of the two-piano team, Marlowe Lane, and together they played host.

At the next lesson I realized that the school program had, in fact, been a test.

"Rose, you have the power to hold an audience. You're beginning to play with authority—I think you ought to play professionally."

This from Rudy! It was the greatest compliment I had ever received. I was speechless. He went on.

"I've found a way for you to have a début recital. The New York Society for Beginning Artists sponsors débuts at the Carnegie Chamber Hall. They cover all expenses."

"Rudy, you could be disappointed."

"I'll take that chance."

"I'll need six months to prepare."

"Fine. You can use some of the things you played at the School."

So it was settled. By now I had managed to buy my first grand piano, a Weber, with one hundred dollars saved from my earnings. Even the family was excited about it. I began practicing six or seven hours a day. It never seemed that long. Time ceases to exist when you bend every fiber of your being toward the perfection of each detail. Again and again you work through a piece, slowly, with your mind on every note until thought and performance are fused and the music flows from you effortlessly. You leave behind things, places, people. Gradually, with concentration, repetition, analysis, and correction, passages that were awkward and difficult become natural and easy. Such a day's practice is a liberating experience. You have a sense of power and catharsis. You feel drained of petty concerns, resentments, restlessness. You are serene, at peace with the world.

So completely was I immersed in my music that I felt no need to go out or to be with people. Dinner with Conway in Manhattan once a week, chats on the phone with Esther, Pill, and Chip, and an occasional concert or play were my only relaxations.

Esther was alarmed. "You ought to be going out—you're too normal, you'll regret it some day."

I knew she was referring to dates with men. For a moment I felt again the pain of the difference between

Début

her opportunities for fun and mine. I wanted them, too. She might be right. Some day when it would perhaps be too late, I might regret this retreat into music, but at the time nothing else seemed as important or satisfying.

I shut out Esther's thought.

The closer it came to début time, the higher mounted my inner commotion. What would the critics say? They had been known to ruin a career with a single derogatory statement. What if I forgot the notes in the middle of a passage—would I be quick enough to cover up? Two nights before the event I had a terrible dream in which I sat at a grand piano, paralyzed before a packed house. My memory was blank, and not one finger could move.

When I reported this to Rudy, he laughed.

"That's a good omen," he declared. "Just keep practicing very slowly, take deep breaths, and think about the beautiful music you want your audience to enjoy."

Papa was indifferent to the début.

"You'll never make any money at it—waste of time. You should have been a lawyer."

Mama preened herself, as always, sure I would be a triumph. How she endured those long hours of practice, day after day, I never understood.

"Mom, this banging must drive you crazy."

"No, no, keep right on. It's important."

Jean shopped with me at Klein's, the working girl's self-service haven. We selected a full-skirted, tight-bodiced red silk jersey with no adornments. Jean hated frou-frous. Price? Five dollars.

On The Night I could eat no supper. As I stood in

the wings waiting to go on, preconcert jitters assailed me: frigid fingers, dry mouth, slight nausea.

Despite Rudy's "You look ravishing," my stomach quivered as I walked on stage. But the powerful Bach-Siloti Chaconne saved me. The fortissimo opening chords demanded all my resources—mental, emotional, physical—as it had in practice sessions. The thorough preparation, brilliant piano, and responsive audience kept me well in orbit, and I knew at the close of the program that it had gone well. There are few sensations in life like those after a good performance, particularly when it has been your début, on which your whole career may depend. You feel a very special kind of high. You want to embrace your audience. You love them for loving your music. Your parachute has opened and you've landed safely. Leontyne Price aptly described the feeling as "the most unsurpassable I can think of, even being with a man."

Rudy was exultant. Instead of flowers, he and Marlowe, now his wife, presented me with Dr. Hays's *How to Be Always Well*.

I was still in bed when Rudy called the next morning. His voice sounded two octaves higher than usual.

"I picked up the paper," he said, "and listen to this:

> At no time during Rose Resnick's recital last night could an uninformed listener have reason to suspect that the young pianist was sightless. Miss Resnick played with complete freedom and surety. Her excellent command of the keyboard enabled her to undertake the most difficult music. And all the while her playing had a versatile, expressive personality.

Début

"And," he said breaking off, "there's a lot more just as good. You see, you're on your way."

By then I was bolt awake. "I liked the first sentence in that newspaper critique best," I said. "Rudy, you had quite a bit to do with all that, you know."

Jean rushed out to buy a paper. Mother made apple strudel to celebrate. Perhaps this would mean professional engagements. But no. That required an agent, an agent required money, and money was nonexistent. That night, reliving it all—the applause, the midnight celebration with friends, the gratifying reviews—I faced the same bleak future. Like the B.A. degree, this stab at a concert career was an illusion; it would lead nowhere.

But before long, Rudy threw down another challenge. He would like me to try out in the biennial National Federation of Music Clubs contest.

"You first try out," Rudy explained, "in this district. There are six in the country; ours consists of New York, New Jersey, and Pennsylvania. Then the winners in the six districts compete in the finals."

"Good heavens, Rudy! Do you really think I'd stand a ghost of a chance?"

"Of course I do. You're just starting. You need lots of exposure. And even if you don't win, you can't tell where it might lead."

It was a terrifying prospect, but I had seen what careful, slow practice could do. Leaning, albeit timidly, on Rudy's faith in me, I began concentrating on the required repertoire.

In the Federation auditions, I felt no nervousness and had no memory slips. I thought it went very smoothly, but I came away certain that another contestant who played a lot louder and faster would be the winner. So when Rudy called to tell me that I would be going to San Francisco as one of the six finalists, I couldn't believe him—it couldn't happen to me! The magnitude of a national competition swept past me. All I could think of was that I was going to California. It sounded so glamorous—the golden west, land of eternal sunshine and unlimited opportunity. Whether I won the contest or not, it was thrilling.

Something Miss Guy once said flashed back in my mind. "Some day all of you must try your wings and go out in the world. You won't always need the Lighthouse." Would this be my time? I wondered.

The Lighthouse buzzed with the news. Chip, now known with more dignity as Ruth, and the Lighthouse public relations director, grabbed me.

"Posy, I'm so thrilled for you. You must get in touch with a friend of mine in San Francisco, Henry Taber. Better still, I'll write him. He's very resourceful and will be a nice guy for you to know."

Pill phoned from her office.

"You lucky bum! Can't you take me with you?"

I laughed. "Lucky nothing, old dear—just a lot of work."

On the evening of my departure, there was a strange air of peace in the house. Mother said, "I know everything will be fine—you'll be a winner and the prettiest player of them all, *picture meine*."

Jean was to see me to the train. When the taxi arrived, we each picked up a suitcase and, to my amazement, Papa took mine out of my hand and carried it out.

Début

"Be careful of yourself," he said. "Who is meeting you out there?"

"Travelers' Aid. Don't worry."

He then further surprised me with a goodbye kiss. Papa's softening up as he gets older, I thought.

In the cab I told Jean I wished she were going with me. The taxi was moving slowly through the evening traffic.

"God, I wish I could shake the dust of this place off my feet." She lit a cigarette. "I get pretty damn sick of these birds that come in the shop—they're only interested in taking you to bed with them."

We sat for a while, saying nothing, and then she said, "By the way, Mr. Gruen is meeting you. Wants to see you off. How come? He always seems such a cold fish."

"He's not really cold. Anyhow, he wants to lend me his portable piano so I can practice on the train. You know, keep my fingers limber."

"I'll take off when he comes—I don't feel comfortable with him. O.K.? And he can walk you to the train."

Rudy was waiting for us at the information booth. He had scarcely greeted us when Jean excused herself, kissed me, and hurried off. I took Rudy's arm.

"You look lovely," he said. "How do you feel?"

"Excited and a bit squeamish. I really appreciate your lending me your little piano."

"I know it will do the trick. It has saved my life many times—helps your memory, you know, as well as your fingers. One porter saw me taking the thing into an upper berth one time. He had watched my fingers going up and down on the keys but he heard no sound. He asked me if it were a Ouija board!"

"I'll probably sleep with the thing. Rudy, what are

your plans for the summer? Adirondacks again?"

"I'm not sure." He hesitated. "I guess I may as well tell you—haven't mentioned it to anyone else—Marlowe and I are having difficulties."

"Oh, no!" I was shocked. At the student classes, held at their Riverside Drive apartment each month, all of us had commented on their ideal relationship. Both were top-flight musicians; both were recognized, successful. Marlowe was as beautiful as she was gifted. What could have gone wrong?

"I'm terribly sorry."

"I think I'd better see you on board. According to my watch, they're due to pull out in a few minutes."

At my seat he stood up the keyboard on one end by the window. The train shuddered.

"All aboard!"

Rudy leaned down.

"Goodbye," he said, "and good luck." He gave me a peck on the cheek. I reached out and touched his face.

"Goodbye, maestro."

When the train began moving, I tried to relax. I was glad the occupant of the upper berth had not come to claim his seat. I reached over to Rudy's silent piano. "You'd better bring me good luck," I told it. Fond memories of my lessons flooded back. I owed Rudy so much. My music was beginning to give me more confidence and possibly a way to earn a living, to say nothing of pleasure and inspiration. Although his manner never deviated from the impersonal, I felt closer to him.

The train was gathering speed. I leaned back in my seat, becoming drowsy as I listened to the rhythmic turning of the wheels. Strains of music drifted through my mind. Then, gradually, I was crossing rough terrain, plunging through deep gorges, passing lonely stretches of desert, curving around tall mountains veiled in mist. Out of the mist emerged shadowy figures, one resembling my teacher. Raising a muscular arm, he pointed to a limitless expanse of sea and sky.

"There," he exclaimed against a crashing crescendo, "there's a big world out there—and it's all yours. All you have to do is go out and claim it!"

A deep, polite voice roused me.

"Excuse me, miss—may I make up your berth?"

[9]

Solo in California

When I stepped off the train in Oakland, the ticket agent made me feel a bit like Cinderella.

"We sent away the Travelers' Aid man," he said. "You won't need him, because the Whitcomb Hotel has sent a car to get you."

The driver explained that pictures and biographies of the contestants had appeared in the newspapers and that the hotel liked to do special things for celebrities. He delivered me to a spacious suite, immediately led me to a grand piano, and after removing some bundles from my arms, put them around three dozen roses. As I gasped, he read the card: "Courtesy of the management."

What an entrance! I was overwhelmed. I was also concerned—it all seemed a little premature.

Solo in California

The advance publicity touched off a whirl of invitations. A new pianist in town, and a blind one at that, was news. Overnight I was flooded with requests to play on the air and for clubs and universities. They were willing to pay between twenty-five and a hundred dollars—a windfall.

The invitation from the University of California at Berkeley to play at the Greek Theater worried me. What would the outdoors mean to tone, dynamics, pedal effects, memory? Would I be distracted by candy-wrappers, birds, automobile horns, the wind? I went over the day before to check the stage setup and found an enormous distance between the wings and the piano. I realized I would have to devise a subtle way to walk on alone. Happily, the stagehand had the solution. To serve as a guide, he attached a thread to a knob at the stage entrance, and running the spool out taut, fastened the other end to the piano bench. I went over the route several times, with the fingers of my left hand (the side away from the audience) lightly touching the thread. On the day of the concert, I walked on and off without incident.

No clammy fingers this time—the sun flooded the stage throughout the whole program. Acoustics were excellent, and I was too busy to notice any sounds other than those coming out of the piano. Everyone, including me, had a very good time.

The contest took place a week after I arrived. Although all went surprisingly well, I didn't win. There was no time, however, for one moment's brooding. Playing dates, newspaper interviews, seeing the city, and meeting new people completely absorbed me.

After lunch the next day, Henny Isaacs, aide to the director of the local Association for the Blind, and her driver dropped in. Henny, whom I judged from her voice to be in her early sixties, said, "Mrs. Quist, our director, is eager to meet you. She asked me to tell you not to hesitate to call Blindcraft if you need any help while you are in town."

They had not been there long when the phone rang. A catarrhal male voice said, "I hope you'll pardon this call. I read about you in the paper. You're Rose Resnick, aren't you?"

"Yes."

"Well, I called to ask if we might be related—that is, my name is Resnick, too—Bernard Resnick."

"Oh, no," I answered somewhat testily. "I'm sure we're not. You see, all my relations are East."

"Well, er—couldn't we meet anyhow? I conduct an Army band at a post in Honolulu and I'm here on leave. There's a concert this afternoon conducted by Walter Damrosch. I'd love to take you to it. It's to be outdoors in Burlingame. It's really a beautiful amphitheater."

The idea of driving somewhere in a strange city with a strange man made me apprehensive.

"Well, thank you very much, but I have some guests here," I said.

"Oh, they could come along. I have a Chevrolet sedan."

"Well, let me ask them. Hold on a minute, will you?" I turned and, covering the mouthpiece, explained the situation.

"By all means," said the driver. "Let him come. We'll look him over and if he seems O.K. we'll say,

'Go right ahead and have fun.' but if we think he looks questionable, we'll say, 'We'd rather you came to tea with us.' "

Half an hour later he arrived. From his handshake and the level and tone of his voice, I sized him up as short and stocky, kind, outgoing, and with a certain attractive dignity. While he talked with Henny, her friend drew me aside.

"He has graying hair," she told me, "and a nice, open face. Really distinguished-looking. You go and have a good time."

On the drive down the peninsula we chatted easily. He seemed not at all embarrassed that I was unable to see, an attitude I had found unusual with new people. When he described things to me—the trees, the bay, the homes, the stadium—he didn't say, "Oh, if you could only see the view!" He just told me what he saw and let me enjoy it in whatever way I could.

I haven't the vaguest recollection of the concert, but I remember vividly that we dined and danced at Roberts-at-the-Beach afterwards. I had expected to feel stiff and self-conscious, but as it turned out, I was utterly at ease. He anticipated my every need: "He's just brought the wine." "Do you like a lot or a little dressing?" It all seemed like the kind of help he would offer any girl. Just having a date after so many months of unmitigated work and with one so attentive, so concerned for my comfort and pleasure, was exciting. I hadn't realized how starved I was for a bit of male companionship.

In parting, Bernard said, "I have two more weeks of leave. May I call you? I'd love to take you out. *The Student Prince* is in town. How about it?"

"Wonderful."

Bernard and I saw each other almost every day. We went to museums, to plays, to concerts, and for walks in the parks and along the beaches near the city. We would have a quiet dinner at some fine restaurant. One day Bernard expressed a desire to learn Braille music. I showed him the letters and how they are used to represent notes and symbols in music. He began to transcribe, by hand, the George Wedge Harmony Book, a gargantuan feat, especially for a novice.

The last afternoon before he was to leave he took me for a drive down the coast. Suddenly, in the middle of a conversation, he said, "Rose, will you marry me?"

I felt a ripple of pleasure and a huge wave of surprise, for whether on Twin Peaks at 1:00 A.M. or in the dark of a theater during a play, his most demonstrative gesture was to reach for my hand. What Mother had told us in our teens now flashed back in my memory:

"When men respect you and want to marry you, they don't do intimate things."

I said, "Bernard, we've only known each other a few weeks."

"I feel as though I've known you all my life," he said, adding with a chuckle, "Besides, you wouldn't even have to change your name."

I said, "Give me a little time, Bernard. Let me think about it." I couldn't give him an answer then. I didn't want to hurt his feelings.

He had lent a glow to my stay in San Francisco. It had been delightful to talk with him about music and the theater. But he had a kind of delicatessen personality. He was shorter than I would have liked; he laughed louder than jokes warranted.

Above all, I could not picture myself as an Army wife. Yet I had felt exhilarated on our dates. It wasn't just that he was a man: he was a friend, a kind person. I valued him as such, but I knew then that he could never be my choice for a lifetime mate. There was no need to hurt him, no need for a reply so soon. Never at a loss for conversation, we slipped into other subjects.

We corresponded for two years. Eventually he found a woman he wanted to marry. "Someone like you," he wrote.

It was now time to pack, and I started half-heartedly, hating to think about New York and teaching again at the Lighthouse.

When the phone rang I ignored it—another caller to say goodbye. I might start bawling into the receiver. Then I straightened my shoulders. This is ridiculous, I thought. I should probably be glad I have a job to return to.

I picked up the phone. It was Mrs. Quist, the Blindcraft director.

"I'm looking for a pianist to accompany the Association's vocal quartet."

I clutched the receiver. A job! Was I hearing right? If she had been in the room, I'd have thrown my arms around her.

"I've been reading your recital notices. I think you'd be ideal on our program. And I'd like you to begin right away, if possible. The pay would be twenty-five dollars a week."

Twenty-five dollars! Manna from heaven! It seemed a fortune!

"I was on the point of leaving, but there's really

nothing that compels me to go back to New York. I'll have to see about a place to live."

"You're welcome to come and stay with me until you get located. Why don't you bring your things over tomorrow, so we can get acquainted? I'll send our driver for you."

"Oh, that's very kind, Mrs. Quist."

"Splendid. I'll be expecting you. Make it around noon if you can."

I could hardly wait to dial Henny's number and tell her the good news. I sent Rudy a night letter, and wired Jean, "Hold everything, pal, I'm a winner after all. Got a radio job. Convey my joyful regrets to the Lighthouse."

[10]

Close-up of a Social Agency

AT MRS. QUIST'S bungalow in the western part of the city near the ocean, Sako, the Japanese maid, took my bags and ushered me to a bearskin-covered sofa before a crackling fire.

"Mrs. Quist will be with you in a few minutes," she said. As I waited, I heard the cuckoo clock chiming eleven, and through a window, a gardener clipping hedges. It was my first visit to a city dwelling with a fireplace and a garden. When I heard a heavy tread coming downstairs, I rose to greet my hostess.

"Well, well, I'm certainly happy to see you. You look younger than I expected. What is it, twenty-one? That's right. You're going to be a lift for Blindcraft.

Grady—do you mind if I call you Grady? Sweet Rosy O'Grady. Let me show you around."

Walking next to her, holding her arm, I judged that she was a large woman, about five foot six or seven, in her 50s, erect, with a firm jaw. (Later, her foreman added large gray eyes, spotty makeup, and straight, close-cropped gray hair.) Her voice was stern, full-bodied, of medium pitch, with a touch of the saccharin at times.

After a brief tour of her combined office and bedroom, and the only slightly smaller room I was to occupy, she asked Sako to bring in coffee and sandwiches and proceeded to fill me in on the organization and the job. She had become interested in "doing something for the blind" because of her handicapped child who had died at the age of five. "I used to bring him to the shop every day and carry him around on a pillow." In the beginning she had gathered together a group of blind men once a month, and fed them ice cream and cake.

"Then one day," she explained, "one of them commented, 'Mrs. Quist, it would be so much better if we could work. Then we could buy our own ice cream and cake.' And so we began a broom shop for just those few men until the Cowell family willed us a fine brick building. There are about thirty men now who make brooms, mops, rattan furniture, and baskets. Pearl Byrd, who's been with me for a long time—you'll meet Pearl and I know you'll love her—visits elderly people, teaches Braille, and helps distribute donated clothing."

Mrs. Quist then talked about the vocal quartet.

"They rehearse," she went on, "at eleven fifteen each morning for about half an hour. Pearl and I sing soprano; Mort, a nice young man, sings tenor; and Bill —I call him Billsie—bass. We broadcast every Thursday over K.J.B.S., a local radio station."

Half an hour a day—this was no job, it was paid recreation. I would have plenty of time to practice, and with luck, to fill engagements.

Just then the phone rang. To my amazement it was Henry Taber, Chip's friend. I hesitated. I'd forgotten all about him.

"How did you know I was here—I mean at Mrs. Quist's?"

"Word gets around these parts pretty fast. Any chance of your getting away from the old biddy for a while today?"

"What—?"

"Oh, never mind, not now. I'd like to show you some of our beautiful countryside—how are you on hiking?"

"I'd love it, but just a minute, I'll have to ask Mrs. Quist if she'd mind."

She said No, but I detected disappointment in her voice.

As Sako cleared away the lunch dishes, I began planning what I would wear for the new date.

Henry arrived promptly at two. After the usual introductory exchanges I asked, "Is your car outside?" Everyone I had met in California had a car.

"Oh, no," he said, obviously taken aback. "I don't see well enough to drive."

I gasped. I had never been out with a blind man, and I was scared.

"But," he went on, "you needn't be concerned—I see well enough to avoid obstacles. Or would you rather we changed our plans?"

I wanted to say, "By all means, let's," but how could I?

Actually, he managed very well on the bus and ferry to Sausalito, then the train to Mill Valley. We talked easily. He was slim, of medium height. I felt the impact of a sensitive, high-strung person with all antennae working.

"To start this safari," he informed me, "we climb one hundred steps to the Dipsea Trail."

After forty of these my legs screamed.

"God, fella, this ain't no hike," I panted. "We're scalin' a mountain!"

"Don't worry, this is the worst of it, really."

The trail, just wide enough for the two of us, led gently upward through groves of eucalyptus, bay, fir, maple, madrone, and redwood trees. The hot sunlight intensified their fragrance. Henry introduced me to poppies, lupine, Indian paintbrush, Scotch broom, wild iris. Now and then tiny waterfalls or brooks splashed at our sides, and we would squat on rocks for a drink, or pause to munch on the fruit Henry had brought along. It all reminded me of Mossyledge.

We fairly loped down the last lap of the mountain to the country road where, since it was already five fifteen, we hitched a ride to the beach. Over French bread, cheese, and wine from Henry's larder, we probed each other's pasts. He was a graduate of the California School for the Blind, now struggling to earn his living as an insurance salesman. He was an angry man, a rabid Republican who deplored government waste, corruption, and intrusion on individual liberty and private enterprise. He was positive America was on the verge of total collapse. "I'd take every last penny out of the bank and just hang on to the cash. When these banks go, they'll just go poof, like a balloon."

He had no good word for religion: "The churches are rich, their parishioners are poor," he declared.

He hated his alma mater and was suspicious of "all institutions that allegedly help the blind."

"Aren't you kind of overgeneralizing?" I suggested.

"Well, name one that's genuine," he challenged.

"I've only had a close-up of the Lighthouse in New York," I said, "and when I was a child it was a beautiful thing, really set us kids on course—physically, socially, psychologically."

"And how much do you know about what you're getting into right now?"

"Nothing, really."

"Well, I'll clue you. Watch out for the old lady you're staying with. Her workers don't trust her."

"How do you mean, Henry?"

"I don't want to discourage you—you'll find out soon enough."

"My responsibilities are only to accompany the radio singers. That shouldn't be too complicated."

"You may come off all right because she can use you. But she considers blind people an ungrateful lot. Isn't that a laugh? She should be grateful to them for providing her with a living."

"I'll only be at the shop half an hour each day. Anyhow, I appreciate the warning."

Before leaving the beach, Henry read my palm and tried to explore other parts of my anatomy. Trying to avoid a wrestling match, I said, "We'd better be heading back. How are you on hitching rides in the dark?"

"That's the best time," he said, undaunted.

In the rumble seat of a rickety roadster we hailed, he wanted to know if I would go home with him.

"I can make just dandy scrambled eggs—with mushrooms and wine."

"I'd jolly well better scramble back to Mrs. Quist's," I said.

It was ten o'clock when Henry deposited me at Mrs. Quist's door.

"Do you mind if I leave you before she comes?" he asked. "I don't want to run into her."

"Not at all."

"Sure you don't want to come home with me?"

I laughed. "No thanks."

I rang the bell. No answer. I rang again—still no answer. This woman must be a deep sleeper, I thought. I tried again, this time leaning longer on the bell—still all quiet. I jangled the bell several times fiercely. No result. I pounded on the door and called out, "Mrs. Quist, Mrs. Quist, it's Rose." Surely she hadn't gone out. After about fifteen minutes of ringing, calling and waiting, I concluded that she must have expected me to return earlier and was angry. I remembered Henry's warning about my new employer.

I suddenly realized that I was totally alone in a strange city. Not a soul was on the street. Every few minutes a foghorn, loud, strident almost like a human groan, petrified me. Wisps of fog wet my hair, face, and clothes.

I thought of Henny Isaacs. She might come to my rescue if—a big if—I could find a telephone.

Descending the five steps of Mrs. Quist's entrance, I followed the stone walkway to the street, taking one

Close-up of a Social Agency

timid step, pausing, then another. Was her house on the corner, in the middle of the block, near another house? I turned left, extending my left hand to scan for obstacles in my path and for clues to what I was passing, and thus gingerly proceeded some twenty steps to a house. Would I wake these people? I had to chance it. I rang. A man came to the door.

"You saved my life," I said trying to sound calm.

"Come in," he said when I had explained my predicament. "Let's phone her."

But the phone call received the same response as had the doorbell. Henny was my only hope.

"Grab a cab and come right over," she said, evincing no surprise whatever at what had happened. Was she being loyal to her boss or professionally discreet? Neither of us discussed it. I was too relieved and grateful to pursue a precarious subject: I wondered if I still had a job.

"Don't worry," Henny said after she had revived me with hot chocolate and cinnamon toast, "I know a good girls' club where there's a piano. Room and board is eight dollars a week."

Next morning she collected my bags at Mrs. Quist's and moved me into the Emanuel Residence. I made a mental note that I would be stuffing seventeen dollars in the bank every week—if, that is, I still had a job!

How would Mrs. Quist react to last night's incident? I was to report to work at half past eleven the following morning. Would she gloss over the episode? I was not without pangs of conscience for what must have seemed like walking out on her hospitality, yet I considered that the punishment had been a bit excessive.

Braced for the showdown, I treated myself to a taxi

for the first rehearsal at Blindcraft. I hadn't admitted it to Henry, but the very name "Blindcraft," obviously adopted for emotional appeal, made me recoil. The four-story brick building was on Howard and Seventh streets, in the industrial part of town. Entering through an enormous metal upswinging door, I found myself in a maze of brooms, caned chairs, mops, and stacks of reed baskets. The air was rank with the sweet, nauseating odor of broom corn. I heard the workers shouting to each other above the clang and thump of machinery on the second floor. A hand-operated elevator teetered, swayed, and squeaked as it brought me (with bruised shins and snagged stockings) past the broom-makers to the third floor. It opened onto a huge barn of a room with blind men caning chairs to the left and, some thirty feet to the right, three members of the quartet assembled around the piano. They greeted me cordially, Pearl jumping up from the piano stool and offering to show me the songs they were working on. At ten past eleven we heard the elevator door roll back and Mrs. Quist walked swiftly toward us, calling out, "Hello, folks. Are we all set to rehearse?"

The moment they heard her voice conversation ceased. No special word for me. I had a sinking feeling as she spread out her music on the piano rack. Apparently there would be no mention of last night. She had elected to pretend it never happened. Certainly I would not bring it up—my job was intact.

The rehearsal was a farce. There was no analyzing, no planning, no correcting. The group merely sang through the numbers, Mrs. Quist following the sheet music, the others singing from memory. With the exception of Mort, they ranged in age from forty-five to sixty-seven.

At quarter of twelve a loud bell announced lunchtime. Mrs. Quist had a batch of clothing she wanted to show Pearl in her office. Bill and Mort insisted I join them and the other workers in the warehouse for a bite.

"We have some swell crab sandwiches, and we got an extra one for you—fifteen cents at the corner store."

The word had gotten around that "Her Nibs" had hired a "New York chick" to jazz up her "crazy combo." They were eager to case her out and give her the lowdown. Eight or ten men gathered around a long table a few feet behind the piles of brooms, mops, and baskets, unwrapping hot dogs or reaching into brown bags brought from home. They wanted to know how Mrs. Quist had found me way back in New York, but even more, they wanted to pour out their feelings about the agency.

They reported that Mrs. Quist had been blacklisted for refusing to let the community chest see her books; that although a patron had willed a fruit ranch for the workers' use on weekends and vacations, Mrs. Quist had appropriated it, claiming it was due her for back pay. Hanky-panky! Not another Meinke, I hoped.

"Haven't any of you ever been there?" I asked.

"Yeah. Her favorites, Pearl and Henny, go there quite a bit, I guess"—this from Tony, a particularly virulent chair-caner, short, Portuguese, with huge hands which, on several occasions, I had a hard time keeping in their proper places.

"She falls for flattery," he volunteered, "and there are some stool pigeons around, too. They're in solid.

They get first pickings when there's work, and when they get in some old rags. Wait—you'll hear the old cronies calling her 'boss.' 'Good morning, boss; where shall I put this, boss?' I sure as heck never call her boss—any old time."

Rebel that he was, Tony was the only worker with enough courage to emigrate from that island of the blind. Completely illiterate, he had made brooms at Blindcraft for twenty-two years. But at his parents' ranch in Hayward, he installed a telephone connecting his workshop with the main house. With a complete set of hand and electrical tools, he built shelves and benches, and did all the home repairs. In World War II, Tony applied for a job at the Alameda Naval Air Station. They started him as a metalsmith at $2.58 an hour, increased it to $2.91, and before he retired sixteen years later, presented him with an award for a time-saving device he had invented.

But Tony was an exception. No other Blindcraft worker had the initiative or courage to leave the sheltered environment, and none were encouraged to do so, not even those who were obviously talented and unsuited to broom work. After rehearsal one day, a slender woman in her thirties came to take my place at the keyboard.

"I spend part of my lunch hour practicing," she explained.

I asked if I might listen for a while and heard not only beautiful piano-playing but equally good singing. Naomi ran through several original songs. She was obviously gifted.

"How did you happen to land in a broom shop?" I asked.

"Oh, it was the only kind of work I could get."

I wondered how she could stand it.

"You must hate it," I said.

As I came to know Naomi better, she confided in me her method of survival—her imaginary companions.

"I call them my 'chosen people,'" she said. "They're truly good company—I mean they do interesting things."

"Like what?"

"All sorts of things. One engineer just got a big contract in Guatemala. And his brother, David, a violinist, has fallen in love with a dancer, and doesn't know she's married. They get pretty involved sometimes."

"Had you ever thought of writing down your stories or showing your songs to a publisher?"

"Not really. It's hard to get things published, and I don't think I'm good enough anyhow."

I wondered why Mrs. Quist hadn't featured Naomi as a soloist on her radio program, but when I asked Naomi whether she would like to do it, she backed off from the suggestion.

"Heavens no," she said, "Mrs. Quist might not like it, and besides, I'm not really that good."

What a waste, I thought, for a person of Naomi's ability to live out her days sorting broom corn. Surely an agency purporting to be "for the blind" should have recognized her talent and at least tried to help her realize her potential.

Obviously the shop-workers were not individuals—like the people under Meinke, they were faceless broommakers, basket-weavers, agency statistics.

Although Blindcraft was far from a musician's dream of fulfillment, it left me time for practice and periodic engagements. I played two or three times a week for clubs, for special occasions such as the mayor's reelection, and on radio. When Mrs. Quist heard about one program on a major station, she insisted that I mention Blindcraft. We almost came to blows over it, because I flatly refused, explaining that I disliked any mention of the blind business when not necessary or relevant—that I wanted to be known not as a blind pianist but as a pianist.

For the most part, however, she treated me very well. I could arrive at rehearsals any time I liked, and she allowed me to pocket the proceeds of a recital I played in the Blindcraft auditorium. Yet I could hardly respect her. Besides all that I had heard and observed, her manner was gruff, her jokes derisive.

"Now Billsie, you aren't really going to eat that chocolate bar. You know you want to hold onto that girlish figure." Or, "Pearl, I do declare, with that feather in your hat you look like the best-dressed woman on Skid Row."

Mrs. Quist's favorite project was arranging for the burial of poor blind workers without families. Blindcraft owned two plots in the Cypress Lawn Cemetery, burying those who could afford to pay in one, the less fortunate in the other. Usually dour, bordering on sullen, she became radiant when discussing the cemetery service.

"Grady," she said one day, "isn't it wonderful that Louis doesn't have to go to a pauper's grave. Blindcraft will take care of all the expenses and he can have a decent place to rest."

The more I heard and saw, the more grotesque seemed the whole operation. Machinery and equipment were antiquated. Because most of the work was done by hand, the prices for Blindcraft products far exceeded those in downtown stores. No wonder the agency was always in the red.

But the workers were the only ones who felt the brunt. Like children who assume roles cast by their parents, they learned to behave as they were expected to: They became docile, resigned, comfortable in a subculture which yielded them a pittance and kept them within its confines, in many cases for a lifetime. Meanwhile, the woven baskets and wicker furniture exhibited in the windows that fronted Howard Street drew sentimental praise from an unenlightened public. They were glad someone was "taking care of those poor blind folks."

"It's amazing what those blind people can do. This place is doing a wonderful job."

How could anyone change such a moribund institution? Where did one begin? Even the board setup was a violation of accepted social-work practice. Besides being the paid executive, Mrs. Quist was the dominant—in fact, the only—acting board member. She was accountable to no one. Who the others were, the public never knew. The agency followed no acceptable criteria for working conditions, held no board meetings, published no policy or financial statements.

It was probably true that these blind people might have been worse off without Blindcraft. But surely people like young Mort, Naomi, and probably others, with encouragement and assistance in receiving training and making contacts, could have made their way in the seeing world. I knew there must be a more effective way to help them realize their potentials and lead more satisfying lives. I wanted to find it, but how could I, a newcomer indebted to Mrs. Quist? It would be like biting the hand that fed me.

In any case, a new challenge in my life took precedence over every other consideration.

[11]

New Eyes in Morristown

"It takes nerve the first time, but once you've tried it you'll wish you had done it long ago."

Henry Taber was on the phone, trying to convince me that I should give up Henny's driver and taxis as a way of getting to and from work and strike out alone. The idea of traveling alone throughout the whole city terrified me. I shuddered at the thought of it. In New York few blind people traveled around independently, certainly no girls.

"How do you do it?" I asked him.

"You just start out, put one foot in front of the other, and eventually you'll get there," he said, totally unmoved by my misgivings.

"How do you avoid bumping into people and things?"

"You just learn to listen. People get out of your way."

"But what about posts? They can't."

"You get so you know by the way sounds bounce back and around you, and the feeling around your face and ears when you're passing posts, buildings, open spaces. Haven't you ever stepped out of your house by yourself?"

"Yes, but only around my block as a kid. I know what you mean about sound echoes. But at home there was always a sister or a friend to take me wherever I wanted to go."

"Well, you've got to stop that nonsense. Look at all the blind people who travel alone all the time. If they can do it, so can you. I'll tell you what: This first time I'll make it easy for you. I want you to meet me downtown for lunch, just you all alone. I'll meet you exactly where the bus stops at Larkin Street, so all you have to do is walk one block to the Haight Street car. Tell the conductor to let you off at Larkin. Really, that's a snap. How about it?"

Reluctantly, not wanting him to think me a coward, I said, "O.K., I'll try it."

"Good. I'll meet you there at noon this Saturday."

As we hung up, I thought, if this works this will be the most important day of my life. But I could not think of Saturday without dread. What if I walked into a moving automobile, banged into a post, stepped off the sidewalk into an open sewer? What a fool I had been to let Henry talk me into it. The old way was so sure and simple. But this was for my own good. It would save me money, make me freer, more independent. But could I really pull it off? Henry must know what he's doing; he wouldn't risk my safety.

Finally the terrible Saturday dawned, and with it heart palpitations. The morning dragged on. I checked my Braille watch at least five times until, as eleven thirty loomed, I realized my first problem was to get out of the club unnoticed. I had had to keep the whole experiment a secret lest people worry, possibly panic or even prevent the plan. I couldn't delay. It was time to open the parachute.

As casually as possible I walked downstairs and out of the front door. I knew the building was some thirty steps from the corner. The street was quiet. I turned left, walked to the corner, paused before crossing, heard nothing moving, and proceeded up Laguna to Haight Street, noticing that the buildings on my right created a different sensation than did the open space on my left. I had a free, slightly giddy feeling. At the corner I paused again to listen for traffic. Hearing none, I crossed to wait for the downtown streetcar. I heard the familiar sound of the car coming; the door opened three or four feet to the right of where I stood, and I hopped on. Extending coins for the fare, I asked the conductor to call out Larkin Street.

"Blind folks don't have to pay fare in this town," he informed me. "The seat right behind is vacant."

"Not like New York," I thought and heaved a sigh of relief. My first hurdle was over.

I stepped out at Larkin Street, almost into Henry's arms.

"Well, Tyke," he grinned, "how was it?"

"It was a revelation, Henry," I said, "a kind of quiet

miracle. Somehow, once I got started I almost forgot to be afraid. Maybe I just had beginner's luck."

"No, it gets easier and easier," Henry assured me.

That first solo was a heady experience. Instead of streets there seemed to be oceans of space around me. My hearing, feet, and skin became antennae. The sound of footsteps ahead of me helped line me up in the middle of the sidewalk. I recognized gas stations, drug stores, shoe-repair shops, restaurants, and cleaning establishments by their smells. The direction of the sun and wind helped keep me on course at tricky, curving corners. I became great friends with mailboxes, poles, planters, fireplugs, and street signs. When I heard cars whizzing by in front of me, I knew the light was red. When all was quiet, I knew it was green. People frequently offered to walk across busy streets with me, and I accepted gladly. Despite the tension, I had a feeling of exhilaration after every trip.

For a year and a half I traveled all over San Francisco alone. Except for an occasional bruised shin from an encounter with a child's bicycle, or scuffed shoes or broken heels from misgauging the height of a curb, I was actually enjoying getting around alone. I became overly confident from time to time and would go whizzing along, letting down my guard until a major bump or serious mishap reminded me to be careful.

At the corner of a downtown street one day, an Irish lady stopped me in alarm.

"Sure'n I was watchin' yer as yer was comin' down the strait, and yer missed an open trap-door by the skin of yer taith. Yer'd better be getting yourself one of them blind dogs."

I chuckled at the idea of a blind dog.

New Eyes in Morristown

Some weeks later I had an even closer call.

A friend had given me a single ticket to the opera. On a brisk San Francisco evening, I strode forth to walk the five blocks north and four east from the club to the opera house. I noticed a bit of gravel underfoot at the fourth crossing but continued on, paying no attention, when suddenly I found myself up to my shoulders in a hole. The shock knocked the breath out of me. Dazed, my heart pounding, my skin crawling, I stood motionless. It was a bizarre landing. I couldn't believe I had no broken bones, no bruises, not even a scratch—just a lot of sand in my hair and down my back. I was too unnerved to move. I had started shaking the sand out of my hair, coat collar, and sleeves when I heard heels clicking towards me and quickly shinnied out of the excavation.

Seeing what had happened, the lady was amazed that I was in one piece. I had a hard time convincing her that I wanted to go on to the opera, to which she kindly accompanied me.

I have no recollection of what they sang that night, but I recall urging the usher to help me hail a cab when it was over.

That night decided it—it was high time to get "one of them blind dogs."

It was in the sweltering heat of a New Jersey July, I began training at the Seeing Eye School. There were seven others in the class: a lawyer, a housewife, a newsdealer, a college student, a girl about to be married, and two schoolmates from Illinois.

We had all come to Morristown expecting to meet

our dogs on arrival, but for two days the only evidence of canines was the barking chorale that greeted the trainer at feeding time. We wondered what was going on. To the barrage of questions, the answers given by the staff were the same: "You'll find out. You'll find out." Only much later did we learn that during the pre-dog days the trainer was observing each student's temperament, sense of direction, coordination, balance, freedom of movement, and reflexes. These observations would help the trainer decide which dog was best suited for each student.

Once he stopped the Illinois girls in the hall.

"Sorry, but I have to split you two up. You must learn to get around the premises independently. If you can't manage the building, how are you going to direct your dogs in a city?"

Suspense ran high. Each of us wondered what his dog would be like: what breed, color, sex, disposition. Would it be a shepherd? Weimaraner? Boxer? Labrador retriever? I, who had never liked dogs and in fact was afraid of them, tried to imagine what it would be like to live with one. How would it fit into my life? What would I do with it in a restaurant, at the market, at the theater? Would people welcome me into their homes with a dog?

Mr. Weeman, the trainer, began by teaching us the obedience commands: "Come," "Sit," "Fetch," "Stay." Each required a distinctive tone of voice and gesture.

In those first practice sessions, Mr. Weeman stood in for the dog. He was at one end of the leash, the student at the other giving him commands. Acting thoroughly intractable, he tested our understanding of how to give commands or use the leash, and our capacity for patience.

After lunch on the third day, the great moment arrived. Mr. Weeman gave each of us a piece of meat and sent us to our rooms to await our new companions. Eager, tense, I sat on my bed for what seemed an eternity. Curiosity blocked out fear. I was concerned only about how the dog would react to me, and whether or not I could cope with her. At last, through my open door I heard Weeman's quick footsteps and a dog's hot-hot panting.

"This is Ilsa," said the trainer, handing me the leash. "She's a tawny shepherd, with beautiful lines and big, alert brown eyes. You two make friends. Just stroke her gently and keep saying, 'That's a good girl.'"

Then he left, saying, "I'll see you at dinner."

Before he had finished the sentence, Ilsa had downed the meat and begun to show plainly that she wanted no part of the new arrangement. Tugging at the leash, squeaking and pulling toward the door, she tried to follow the man who, until that moment, had been her master.

So there we were, Ilsa and I, alone with each other. How does one converse with a dog? Trying to calm my forlorn new friend, I ventured, "You're a good girl. You're a beauty." I stroked the tall satin ears, the noble head, but she twirled and paced back and forth, restless and confused in her new abode.

After an hour of frustrated "You're a good girl," and petting, she seemed a bit quieter, tolerating but not really accepting me. I asked, "Ilsa, how would you like to live in San Francisco?" She seemed to be listening.

I tried one of the obedience commands. "Ilsa, sit."

She paid no attention. I repeated the command. I might have said it in Greek. She wasn't taking orders from this new character. How long, I wondered, would it take for that pup to realize she was to obey my commands?

As the afternoon dragged on, I was sure Ilsa thought me a hoax. I could never convince this dog that she had a new mistress.

That night, when eight students and eight dogs gathered round the dinner table, we braced ourselves for bedlam. Despite all my efforts to sound authoritative, Ilsa, tied to my chair, spent most of the time walking to the end of the leash, trying to chat with other dogs under the table, or sitting bolt upright, drooling and pointing at my plate.

"Say, Resnick," the college student teased, "why don't you make a recording of 'Ilsa, down, Ilsa, down?' Save you a lot of breath."

Mr. Weeman tried to help.

"Just give her the command Down as though you meant it. Jerk the leash down at the same time."

But nothing kept Ilsa down that night.

After dinner I met Mr. Humphrey, head of the school.

"How long does it take," I asked in desperation, "for these dogs to get it into their heads that you mean business when you give them a command?"

"You're probably getting impatient and showing it in your voice," he said. "You can't control the dog until you control yourself. And are you remembering to thank your dog when she does the right thing with 'that's a good girl'? That's the most important part of the whole training."

Eliot S. Humphrey, an authority on animal breeding

and training, was the moving force behind the Seeing Eye School, the first of its kind in the country. Having grown up with a blind brother, he understood the problems and capabilities of the blind. His power of analysis and lack of sentimentality helped set the school policy and training on a high plane.

Jack, as we knew him, was never at a loss for spicy stories or quips. When people asked why he took up this work, he said, "The more I see of people, the better I like dogs."

Interesting visitors were always dropping in for lunch. One time Jack said he expected Alexander Woollcott. "He's like the measles, you know—apt to break out anywhere."

He told us once about losing a job in California because he wasn't a native son. "You all know what native son is, don't you? The gold-seekers came in forty-nine; they met the dancing girls in fifty; then there were native sons."

Jack had herded cattle, trained and traded horses, traced inherited characteristics in German shepherds. He was instrumental in formulating the policies and procedures for all future dog-guide training.

Jack initiated the rule that all trainers must perform the activities of daily living—bathing, shaving, dressing, eating, and walking with the dog—under blindfold for one month. During one such orientation session, Jack claimed he had taken moving pictures of the head trainer putting the harness on the dog's rear end.

For three months before the student arrives, the trainer works with the dog in harness, teaching her the core of her guiding work: to obey the commands "right," "left," and "forward." It is the student who must direct his dog, and equally important, he teaches her to stop at any change of level.

Many people have the impression that one just gets on the end of a leash and follows the dog around. To them I point out that if I did that, I would be forever chasing another pup, or rolling on the grass.

One day, on my way downtown, a lady asked, "How is it that that dog always takes you wherever you want to go? I suppose you just give him the name and address, and he takes you there."

I couldn't resist.

"Oh yes," I said, "and if I don't know it, I just tell the dog to look it up in the phone book."

They tell a story at the Seeing Eye about a trainer who once outraged a bystander for correcting a dog who failed to stop at a curb with a sharp jerk of the leash and a loud No.

"That's a terrible way to treat an animal," she shrieked. "You ought to be ashamed of yourself."

"Madame," he replied, "this dog is going to be responsible for the safety of a blind person. If the dog fails to stop at the curb, it might cost the student his life."

Our schedule at Morristown was grueling: up at six, dog-walking at six thirty, breakfast at seven, first trip into town with trainer and dogs at nine, second trip at two, dog-feeding at five, dog-walking at five fifteen, dinner at six, lecture on care and feeding of dog at eight, dog-walking at ten, fall into bed as soon thereafter as possible.

As I took over Ilsa's feeding, grooming, and walking, the obedience improved. On the fifth day, we were ready for our first route, a quiet street with no obstacles in the way. Ilsa's size, her strong, swift gait, and her decisive movements made her easy to follow. We flew along. I'll never forget the excitement of that first walk. Something inside me seemed to expand. I had a sense of unimagined freedom.

On all routes in the training Mr. Weeman followed from several yards behind, close enough to check her for accuracy and obedience to correctional commands, me for posture, correct grasp of the harness, immediacy of response to the dog's subtlest movements, and clarity of voice and gesture in giving directions to the dog.

At the corner of the first street, Mr. Weeman caught up with me. "Have you noticed you're stepping on Ilsa's paw from time to time? You're not keeping your feet straight ahead. Turn your toes in, Miss Resnick."

Learning to trust my dog was an experience of continuing revelation. We were walking briskly along a sidewalk one day when Ilsa stopped suddenly. Why in the middle of a sidewalk, halfway down the block?

"Ilsa, forward," I commanded.

Ilsa planted her feet and would not budge. Again I gave the command, and again not a stir. I reached forward with my right hand, touched a car in front of us, and quickly corrected myself. "That's a good girl," I said, thanking my dog as Jack had emphasized.

I soon learned why people using guide dogs must have quick reflexes. We were walking along another sidewalk when a car turned close in front of us and zoomed into a garage that I didn't realize was there. Ilsa stopped with lightning speed.

From the quiet streets we graduated to a shopping center. Now Ilsa had to avoid groups of shoppers, parked cars, boxes and carts in front of markets. I neither knew nor thought about what we were passing; Ilsa circumvented all with ease. Next we worked the country roads, then areas under construction, buses, and department stores. The dogs took us through revolving doors, down crowded aisles, up in elevators.

In one store, Ilsa and I had gone up to the sixth floor to look at knitting yarns, and, when I had made my purchase and had walked to the elevator to take us down, I reached out to push the button and noticed that the door was open. I gave the command, "Forward." Ilsa stood motionless. Now what? I wondered. Again, I said, "Ilsa, let's go—forward."

Suddenly Mr. Weeman, still monitoring our every move, called out, "Stand still—you're in front of an open elevator shaft." A chill ran through me. I stood *very* still!

Finally we were ready for the acid test: city traffic. We worked as a team—Ilsa watching, I listening. I knew from my solos that racing motors mean Stop, and their idling, Go. (Dogs, who are color-blind, can't distinguish between red and green lights.) Mr. Weeman turned us loose with "I'll meet you at Eighth and K streets. You're on your own."

After watching us work in heavy traffic, Mr. Weeman decided that we would be safe anywhere. On the way back to the school in the station wagon, he said, "Well, Rose, I guess you are ready to graduate."

A lump rose in my throat. Ilsa was my dog at last.

Because I was so close to New York, I wanted to visit the family. Since the first Seeing Eye guiding must be done in the home area, Mr. Weeman arranged to have Ilsa shipped to San Francisco. I wept at having to leave her for even a few days.

She proved so excellent a guide that on one of our

nightly walks around the block a man caught up with me and said, "Pardon me, miss, but I must tell you that I've been watching you for some time, and I think it's wonderful of you to take that poor blind dog for a walk every night."

[12]

The Search Begins

Before leaving New York, I managed to sandwich in a lesson with Rudy. Somehow from the moment I entered the studio he seemed different: more informal, even friendly.

"What a tan!" he greeted me. "You look marvelous." Instead of sitting at the second piano as usual, he drew up a chair next to mine and asked in detail about Morristown, my job, and life in California. Then he shocked me with the news that he and Marlowe were divorced.

"You were such a beautiful duo," I said. "How could that happen?"

"It was little things, things that would sound silly if I mentioned them now—we'd decide to go downtown by subway and get in the street and she'd insist on a cab. And there were more important things, too. We'd decide to do a certain passage one way while we were working

The Search Begins

on it at home; we'd get out on the platform and she'd change the whole thing."

"And you couldn't arrive at any understanding, couldn't talk it out?"

"I suppose we could have gone on forever if we hadn't succumbed to convention. Concert pianists shouldn't marry; at least I never should have."

When I got back to the Emanuel, the girl at the desk handed me my mail. The envelope with the crooked stamp accelerated my pulse a beat or two. I knew it was a letter from Rudy. I thanked the Lord that my roommate was home to read it for me. Although Rudy had intimated that his marriage was a mistake and that he was well rid of it, his letter revealed quite different feelings:

> As you can imagine, my recent divorce has brought on one of my periodic spells of depression. My only consolation is in yoga and Eastern philosophy. I hope the Bay Area is properly appreciating you and that you have many opportunities to inspire audiences as your playing did me.
>
> I sent you some books last week. Let me know what you think of them.
>
> *Salaam Aleikum,*
> *Rudy*

He apparently approached his letter-writing as he would a music score, using green ink for worldly sentiments, blue for spiritual thoughts and red for emphasis, all copiously sprinkled with dashes and exclamation points. He embellished his signature with a huge R, ending in a C clef. He explained that this was a kind of mandala, a symbol of "spiritual exaltation, music of the spheres, peace, beauty, and wisdom."

His despondency, I was sure, was typical of an artistic temperament. I tried to divert him in my reply:

> How very kind of you to send those books. I particularly enjoyed Nehru's *Discovery of India*, for I agreed with his attitude toward life and religion. "I prefer the open sea," he says, "with its storms and tempests to the safe anchorage from doubt and mental conflicts. Nor am I interested in the afterlife. I find the problems of this life sufficiently absorbing to fill my mind."
>
> Nehru seems to be the synthesis of East-West thinking. Instead of rejecting life, he accepts and tries to understand and improve it.
>
> "Most religious men," he writes, "are far more concerned with their own salvation than with the good of society."
>
> I admire his capacity for meaningful detachment, not just making a vacuum of himself but using his powers here and now for the betterment of his people.
>
> About depression, Dr. Johnson advises: "When you are solitary be not idle, when you are idle, be not solitary."
>
> I do hope, Rudy, that by the time this reaches you, your vitality will have returned. Perhaps you need to do what I did a while ago—get a medical checkup. The doctor declared me anemic, low in red blood cells. My only symptom was a feeling of terrible lassitude and depression.
>
> Incidentally, Dr. Lazar is a music patron, entertains Schnabel at his home when he is here on tour.

The Search Begins

Lazar says one has to be a gourmand to be a good pianist, that both Brahms and Chopin were gourmands. "Yes," I replied, "and Brahms got the gout and Chopin died of consumption."

He corrected me: "Chopin died of syphilis—he got it in Paris. The girls consumpted him."

This exchange was the beginning of a long, often widely spaced correspondence. His flights into mysticism, his many travels, and his increasing recognition as a pianist and composer made his letters fascinating. Each time one arrived my heart skipped a beat or two.

Early in 1937, one year after I had come to California, the Blindcraft broadcasts came to an end. Mrs. Quist claimed it was because she refused to join the union, but I suspected the quartet's rating might have had something to do with it.

The loss of my only regular source of income brought me to grips with the need of a steady job—I had to have something I could count on. Opportunities to play, numerous at first, were now sporadic. The Fontainebleau and Manhattan School diplomas should, I thought, qualify me to teach somewhere. Perhaps the California School for the Blind in Berkeley could use me. But when I went to see the superintendent, he told me to come back when I had my teaching credential and master's degree.

Encouraged by Dr. French's willingness to hire me and with no other apparent avenue of security, I enrolled as a parttime student at the University of California at Berkeley. My savings and occasional paid engagements would see me through a year or two.

What a contrast the university was to old Hunter! Ilsa and I loved to tramp along those tree-lined paths, broad lawns, streams, flowerbeds, and shrubs, pausing to answer questions about her from students who became our friends.

During the two years I commuted to the campus, the monstrous shadow of World War II began to break on America. Along the avenues on the way to class, Hitler's hysterical haranguings blared from radios. Newspapers told of innocent people dragged from their beds, robbed, and slaughtered. Had reason completely left the planet? I wondered how students could go about their business not heeding, not caring, immersed in football or fraternity parties. My heritage, no doubt, explained my own haunting concern.

But everyone lives his life in compartments, and although this was a disturbing part of my university experience, I thoroughly enjoyed my studies.

Since we were allowed a selection of courses, I chose Choral Literature with Randall Thompson, the Beethoven Quartets with Albert Elkus, and Contemporary Music with Roger Sessions.

One of the most challenging of the requirements for the teaching credential was a semester of practice teaching, the actual conduct of classes under the supervision of regular teachers. In my assigned classes, French and Harmony, I used a seating plan to facilitate roll-taking. I kept Braille as well as typed records of attendance, assignments, examination questions, and grades. The two best students in each class helped correct blackboard work and read me quizzes for grading.

I told the students they would be on their honor during examinations; that I hoped I would not find it necessary to resort to giving each row of students a different set of questions. I never had to use this device. In fact, discipline was no problem. Ilsa remained motionless under my desk.

It appeared that things were going quite satisfactorily, for by the end of the first year I was initiated into Alpha Mu, the honorary music society, and Pi Lambda Theta, the honorary education society.

So when my final grade in practice teaching from Dr. Sampson, director of education, came back a *B* instead of an *A*, I was demolished. With the competition for a job I would face, I felt I had to rate an *A*. I presented myself at his office for an explanation.

"Miss Resnick," he said, "no matter how well you know your subject, discipline your classes, or please your supervisors, it stands to reason that you couldn't possibly teach as well as a person who can see."

There it was again. You can't see, therefore you're incompetent, regardless of what the records show.

Between sobs, I blurted out, "You're not fair. I should be graded on the basis of my performance as a teacher, not as a handicapped person—unless my being blind prevented the students from learning what they were supposed to in my class."

It fell on deaf ears. The *B*, coupled with his attitude, was a death knell to my chances in competition with seeing applicants for teaching jobs.

I waited several months without a single call from the university placement office, then went back to Dr. French at the School for the Blind. He only laughed.

"I'd have to shoot one of my teachers," he said, "to give you a job."

Not another comment. How flippant, how callous!

Was he like this with his students? I was crushed. He might be my last hope.

But I answered a notice in a Braille magazine announcing an opening at the North Carolina School for the Blind. I asked the university placement office to send the superintendent my letters of recommendation. The superintendent replied that he hired only his own graduates. His letter, however, contained a golden surprise: my complete confidential file, letters which should of course have been returned to the university. They exceeded my most optimistic expectations. At least I could be sure that my references would not keep me from landing a job.

Not long afterwards, John Dodd, then head of the Bureau of Vocational Rehabilitation, sat next to me at a social worker's luncheon. He said he knew every superintendent in the state and would send my résumé to all of them.

Months passed without a word from the bureau. Finally, a rehabilitation counselor came to see me and recommended that I move to a small town and develop a class of private pupils. But how could I, without the capital for furniture, a piano, rent, or even the major move? Interesting way of rehabilitating people, I thought—just get them to move out of the area.

One night a friend in whom I had confided about my frustrating search for a job invited me to a lecture at the public library.

"It's La Roche," she said, "she's fabulous—gives courses in Personal Applied Psychology. She's accomplished miracles for people."

"I've had Applied Psychology," I told her. "What I need is applied money."

The Search Begins

"But seriously, Rose," Kate urged, "she has salvaged marriages, made people well, helped them achieve in all kinds of situations. If you follow through on her course, I know she can help you. She's worth hearing anyway."

To please my friend, I went.

La Roche's appearance on the platform created a stir. "Oh, stunning." "Striking, isn't she." "Is she Negro?" "American Indian, I believe." "What a figure!" "She must be six feet." And more about her smart dress and jewelry. Her talk was largely what I expected —a sales pitch for students—but her manner was pleasantly persuasive and most of her audience came away captivated.

Kate insisted that we go backstage and meet THE La Roche. "Oh Miss Resnick, Kate's told me so much about you and your music. And I suppose she's told you about my work." We were into the course. "It covers financial planning, diet, self-understanding, building self-confidence . . ." On and on. I had better stop her, I thought, before she makes the first appointment.

She proposed that we exchange piano lessons for the P.A.P. course.

Ready to try anything, I accepted her offer. She didn't practice, and I didn't land a job, but one of her techniques indeed proved cathartic.

"Most of us carry around fear, envy, resentment—feelings we've repressed that prevent peace of mind. It's just as important to rid ourselves of these," she stressed again and again, "as to get rid of our body waste every day."

I saw no connection between my repressions and my

goals, but I was glad to try her method on the feelings of anger and resentment toward my father that had lodged and churned around in my subconscious since childhood. La Roche insisted I write him off—by putting a sheet of paper in the typewriter and pouring out everything I felt about him, without concern for form, language, or coherence.

The first time I tried it, I could hardly type. My memory ached, the tears flowed on almost every one of forty pages. I relived his treatment of Mother, his nagging tirades that pushed my brothers and sisters into hasty marriages, his rages that terrified and drained all of us, his sullen moods that made home sordid, dreary. During the second try, twenty pages, I cried only intermittently. The third time, a lot of the poison had gone out of me. In fact, at page ten, I stopped and tore it all up. Now, instead of virulent surges of gall, I realized that he actually had punished himself. He was always deeply unhappy. Even his jokes and stories had never won him friends. His children fled his house. He was trapped by his own passions. Now, instead of bitterness, I could think of him with pity, almost forgiveness. After all, he had come out of a Russian ghetto where—coming to the defense of villagers who were oppressed, cheated, humiliated—he felt important, almost a hero. Here in America he was anonymous. He could find no avenue of fulfillment or expression in the urban environment. And—I had to admit it—he and Mother had nothing in common—he interested in politics, in world affairs, in what he found in his daily newspapers; she only able to talk about her children and her home. He must have been plagued with the need to provide adequately for his

The Search Begins

family. Now, looking back, I could understand and sympathize.

Ironically, that year—1943—he died. He strode out of the house one day to buy himself a new suit, and an hour or so later he collapsed in the street and was brought home by strangers. Sarah summoned the doctor who had attended him for high blood pressure over the years. He cited heart failure as cause of death. Papa was eighty-five.

At the time, Sarah and Mother were living on the fifth floor of a Brooklyn apartment house. In one of her letters, Sarah described Mother's reaction to a painting job on her apartment. "When the man got through, Mama said it looked as bad as ever. So she climbed up on a ladder and painted over the whole job. She's eighty-three now. The other day she insisted on washing all the windows—just sat on the sills, with no fear."

Mother was still sighing, "If only God would give me a few years to live without him!" She got her wish, surviving him by eight peaceful years. She still insisted on doing her own early-morning shopping. On a day of ice and sleet, as she stood waiting to cross the street, a truck struck her, killing her instantly.

The news was sudden and stabbing. Having been away from home so long, I had pictured her as going on and on in the manner of her ancestors, most of whom had lived into their upper nineties. I thought of her years of silent suffering, how all of us but Sarah had left, rarely visiting the old home. I saw the small, sturdy figure bent over the high tub of clothes, smelled again the perennial Fels Naphtha soap, and heard again her plaintive singing. Again, with my Braille book in my lap, I sat with her at the window, she darning a sock or sheet, or crocheting a cap for one of us, catnapping between stitches, watching life go by. I thought of all those years of prodigious labor, and of how, after her children had left, she had asked nothing of them. Her life baffled me. I felt a numbing sadness. I was glad that her death had been quick and painless. I shed no tears, for Mother was still, and always would be, very much alive inside me.

[13]

From Bach to Boogie

Knowing how much Jean hated New York, I tried in my letters to persuade her to come West. Finally, right after I had finished at the university, she decided to make the move. She had hardly set foot in San Francisco when she met the man who was to be her second husband, a Baptist Dutchman.

The difference in their backgrounds created a rocky marriage, but Frank taught Jean many skills and elevated her standard of living. The one thing they had in common was bottomless wells of energy, all of which they poured into Lanlay, an all-purpose cosmetic created by Frank—so pure, he claimed, that you could drink it. Together they built the business, working day and night out of a twenty-five-dollar-a-month rented store. Frank sold; Jean bottled, packed, and shipped. She learned to type and handle the books. In time, they hired a man to do Jean's work, and she joined Frank in countrywide travels during which Frank taught Jean to bowl, ice-skate, and ski. In another five years the product sold throughout the United States, South America, Germany, Japan, and Formosa.

When Jean first arrived, I had had my fill of boarding. It was time to take the plunge and try to manage my own apartment. Jean and I found a high-ceilinged studio with a large living room, a fireplace, and a tiny kitchen, near a park, handy for exercising Ilsa. But the landlady had misgivings about renting to a blind girl with a piano (borrowed from a friend) and a dog to boot.

"Supposing something happens to her?" She addressed Jean as though I were not present. "Who will take care of her? How can she use a stove? She might get hurt."

I assured her that an electric stove was perfectly safe and—I demonstrated with one of the switches—very simple to use. I explained that Ilsa gave me complete independence in traveling about the city. To further allay the landlady's fears, Jean promised to be a frequent visitor. She finally accepted me, but I knew I was on probation.

The first months were a crazy comedy of errors. One night I waited almost an hour for an ear of corn to cook. Just as I was about to give up, a friend dropped by and informed me that I had covered only half of it with water. Another time I thoroughly baked a casaba melon, mistaking it for a banana squash. Jean consoled me by admitting that the first time she cooked asparagus, she boiled the bottoms and threw away the tops.

At first, I identified canned goods by putting fruit on one shelf, vegetables on another; coffee and tuna were simple enough to recognize by their size and shape.

But one night, for a topping on vanilla ice cream, I began pouring what I thought was pineapple but turned out to be creamed corn. From then on, I took the time to label cans in Braille. I bought a Braille timer, like any other except for notches at five-minute intervals, but relied mainly on my nose or the feel of food under a fork to know when it was done. I sent away for Braille cookbooks, assiduously read the recipes, then stored them in the bookcase or gave them away.

Jean was marvelous to me in a maddening sort of way, as bossy and full of admonitions as ever. "You're going to ruin the furniture if you keep those shades up all the time." "Don't ever put newspapers on a light couch. The print comes off on everything." "You're not getting that kitchen stove really clean—you have to get behind the stove and refrigerator."

For my birthday, Jean declared, "You're getting a new toaster whether you want it or not—this thing's ready for the garbage." I would have preferred a sweater, but Jean had spoken.

Her nagging was maddening, but in many ways she was a godsend. She had a key to the apartment, and often I came home to find the kitchen and bathroom floors scrubbed and groceries replenished. Of course, for days there was an exasperated hunt for things in drawers and medicine cabinet—everything had been organized. I took to hiding things I most used. As a last resort, I gave in and learned to fold things the "right way," which meant the way they looked neat and wouldn't crease.

Three boys from Alabama moved into the apartment next door. Two days later, they complained that I didn't practice long or often enough. The one who apparently kept house for the trio dropped by one morning.

"They call me Connie, short for Conrad," he said. "May I come in for a minute?"

Before I could utter a word, he was in the living room.

"I have red hair and hazel eyes, and I'm five foot eleven and slim. We love your playing—we stop everything and sit with our ears to the wall."

"Thank you. Sit down, won't you?"

"It's almost lunchtime. People get to know each other better over a meal. I brought along some shrimp for a salad and a lemon pie I made last night."

"Good heavens, I'll play for you any time."

And while he fixed the salad and I set the table, he claimed he could whistle bass and soprano at the same time and proceeded to prove it. He informed me that he loved perfume and nice furniture, cooking and sewing. Before he left he put up a hem for me and fixed a shade and the vacuum cleaner. He was so natural, so kind, you couldn't help liking him. He felt no embarrassment about his voice, his interests, and his skills. You accepted them as part of his gentle and amusing personality. I missed him sorely when he and his buddies moved away.

By 1940 my savings had dwindled to two hundred dollars. The cost of the apartment, food, clothes, and Ilsa's care and feeding were frightening. Unless I found a steady source of income, I would soon have to apply for Aid to the Blind. A devastating thought!

At my wit's end, I snatched at every straw in the wind. For three months I sold ads for a music and dance magazine, earning forty-five dollars in commissions. For two dollars a session twice a week, I taught music appreciation at the YWCA. This job, however, paid another kind of dividend. The head of the Y Business Girls, Bernice Foley, asked me to write music to a skit she planned for a spring festival. It touched off a collaboration in writing popular tunes that continued for years. Bernice said her lyrics came to her while she brushed her teeth.

"They're just as good as anything on the Hit Parade," our friends insisted. So we sent off a batch to a dozen or more publishers. Back they all bounced, unopened. The gist of all replies was the same: "We do not use unsolicited material. We have our own writers."

Undaunted, we continued our hobby, finally winning a twenty-five-dollar award for our song "Your Lips Touched Mine," submitted in a contest on Hedda Hopper's radio program, *Hollywood Showcase*. At the producer's request, I flew to Hollywood to accompany the singer and orchestra on the show.

The only time I got close enough to talk to Miss Hopper was in the restroom after the rehearsal.

"My friends will be thrilled to know that I met you," I ventured.

"Yes, and you can tell them we both peed in the same toilet," Hedda quipped.

To remind San Francisco that I was available for engagements, I decided to give a recital at the Century Club, capacity two hundred. With the help of some of the socialites I had met in the contest days, I netted four hundred dollars. Next morning, I trembled to hear the critique in the papers, but again I was lucky: "surprising virility," "subtle phrasing," "beauty of tone."

This bolstered my confidence enough to audition for soloist in the National Broadcasting Company's

Sunday night series, conducted by Meredith Wilson. He scheduled me to do the first movement of the Grieg Concerto—no pay, but it was a network broadcast and would mean publicity and prestige. I immediately notified my family, my friends, and—with shivers—Rudy.

My only previous experience in playing with an orchestra had been at Manhattan School of Music graduation night. Heard coast to coast, with Rudy listening to every note, the performance would have to be flawless. The prospect put me into more than the usual state of agonizing suspense. But somehow, on the night of the performance, once into the opening passages, I slipped into my usual state of nirvana and disappeared into the music itself, buoyed along by the sea of instruments around me.

We had just finished. The players were surrounding and congratulating me when a voice boomed over the mike, "Miss Resnick, long distance."

It was Rudy.

"Rose, that was magnificent."

"Really? I wouldn't know. As usual, I was unconscious the whole time."

"You were fine. You should feel wonderful. How are things going out there?"

"Terribly, I seem to be hitting nothing but dead ends."

"Why don't you try for a radio program? They use live talent, you know. Tonight should give you a good sendoff."

"You mean for a regular program? Doesn't that take a huge repertoire?"

"You can handle it, I'm sure. We'll talk about it when I see you."

"Rudy! You mean you're coming West?"

"I'm hoping to. There's a short break in a spring tour I'm considering. I may be able to stop over in San Francisco—I'll let you know."

Next spring was a long way off, but the possibility of seeing Rudy lifted my spirits as I continued job-hunting. Late one night, casting about for a way to keep my N.B.C. contact alive, a program idea flashed into my mind: the story of America in folk music. Using early hymns and spirituals, American Indian chants, songs of the rivers and canals, railroads, cottonfields, chain gangs, and cowboys, on up through ragtime, blues, and jazz, one could make a colorful radio series. A week later, with Ilsa in harness and sample script under my arm, I set off to see John Nelson, then program director of the San Francisco N.B.C. outlet.

"We follow a standard procedure," he said, "with all new ideas. We require that you sign over all rights to N.B.C. This is to protect us from suit, should the network ever produce a similar show or series." I saw no reason not to sign.

Weeks passed without a word from Mr. Nelson. Finally, knowing the notorious inaccessibility of radio program directors, and unable to contain my curiosity any longer, I called him.

"Your idea is more expensive than we can afford," he said, "but how would you like to do a sustaining show—just playing the piano and chatting with the announcer, say a fifteen-minute program?"

"Sustaining" meant without pay, but the possibilities such exposure would open up were certainly worth it. I would be heard regularly all over northern California.

If it went well, it would be a feather in my professional cap. It might even bring paid engagements.

The show began in June 1941. I felt as relaxed behind the mike as on the stage with the old Lighthouse Players. There was a certain fascination in just being around a radio station and in talking to and hearing from all those people out there. Fifty or sixty letters came in each week, most of them very friendly and flattering, but the station considered that response a mere trickle. Bach, Mozart, and Rachmaninoff were all right, but what most listeners wanted was jazz. I had played by ear since childhood but had never cultivated a truly professional popular style, so I compromised by making popular arrangements of the classics and arranging popular tunes in the classical vein. I found it great fun. Paderewski's Minuet became "Paddy's Minuet in Modern Dress," the quartet from Rigoletto became "Rigoletto Boogie," and "Pistol-Packin' Mama" appeared in the style of Chopin, Haydn, and Brahms. I was sure Rudy would call the whole business the decline and fall of a classical musician, but it was "commercial" and at the moment, that was the key to success.

As the year wore on, however, news of the war crowded the airwaves. A day, a half day, sometimes just an hour before my show was to start, the producer would call to say it was canceled, preempted by news. So it came as no surprise when, in November, my program was terminated.

Hitler was on the march and gaining, his violent ravings still exploding on the air. People said it couldn't happen here, yet an unspoken dread that it could lurked throughout the land. I think there was almost a sense of relief, grim as it was, when America became involved.

From Bach to Boogie

Inevitably everyone felt the impact of the war one way or another. Shipyards sprang up all over the Bay Area. Women became welders, riveters, assembly-line workers, bus-drivers. People grumbled about gas rationing and soaring prices. Within a few months, men returned from the war blinded, shocked, crippled. Hospitals bulged. Volunteers thronged to blood banks and U.S.O.'s. I couldn't give blood because I weighed less than 110 pounds, so I was delighted when the Army YMCA asked me to join a troop that put on variety shows for the blacked-out Army camps around the bay.

One request was from the psychiatric ward in Dibble Hospital in Palo Alto. What, I wondered, would I play for men on a locked ward? Classics might bore them. Boogie, so popular at the time, might stir them up. On the way to the program I decided to open with the Rhapsody in Blue, then simply ask them to call out their requests. I found them as attentive and enthusiastic as any audience I had ever played for. They asked for "Clair de Lune," Moonlight Sonata, Schubert's Serenade—not one request for jazz. Why was I surprised? Just ignorance, quite the usual attitude towards people we know nothing about. They gave me new insight into the power of music as therapy, a tool used since the war by many mental institutions.

Equally memorable, though for very different reasons, was the program at Letterman General Hospital's ward for the blind.

The dignified, soft-spoken supervising nurse greeted me.

"Haven't I heard your name before—on radio, I believe?"

"Probably."

"Of course. It was on N.B.C. one night before I went on duty. The patients are in for a treat."

At the close of the program, she asked if we couldn't meet sometime.

"There are a lot of questions you could help me with about newly blinded soldiers."

Nina was a shy twenty-three when we met. From her mother, who had worked as a model, she inherited perfect posture, blue eyes, and blond hair. Five foot six, poised, she had the unmistakable competent look of a nurse.

When she was twelve years old, her mother died from an overdose of gas in a dentist's chair. The responsibility of keeping house for her father and youngest brother then fell upon Nina. After high school she went into nurse's training, then enlisted in the Army Nurse Corps. At Letterman, she worked first on the ward for the blind, then as supervisor of the psychiatric ward.

Mack, one of her patients, had more than a patient's regard for his supervising nurse. In combat in the South Pacific he had lost part of his forehead, the bridge of his nose, and both eyes. After watching a few of my techniques, Nina had taught him adapted ways of pouring liquids, cutting meat, measuring, dialing a phone, and so on. He had worked on a newspaper in Maine when he could see, and Nina assured him there was no reason why he couldn't continue in the same profession. When the doctor declared him ready for a night on the town, he asked her to go out with him, but deeming it unwise to deviate from her professional relationship, she declined. Naturally sensitive to his new circumstance, Mack misinterpreted her refusal.

"I know why you won't go out with me. You don't want to be seen with a blind man," he said.

Thereupon Nina tossed convention to the winds.

"Mack, that's ridiculous. Just for that, you've got yourself a date. And it had better be good."

And very good it was. Mack took her to dinner at the Fairmont and then to Noel Coward's *Blithe Spirit*. When they arrived at the theater, they joined the audience in a salute to the flag and "The Star-Spangled Banner." Nina noticed tears running down Mack's face.

"Excuse it, Boots," he whispered, using her Army nickname. She had a hard time holding back her own tears.

On the psychiatric ward, 250 G.I.'s a week were streaming in with battle fatigue from the South Pacific. Few of Nina's predecessors had been able to tolerate for more than a few months the hostility, violence, hallucinations, and withdrawal behavior of those tormented patients. I would call Nina from time to time and hear bloodcurdling shrieks.

"What on earth is going on over there?" I asked.

In a completely unruffled voice she would say, "Oh, that's just one of the patients."

She was a natural for the job. Using intuition, common sense, and patience, she often solved problems that stymied the psychiatrists. In the process of admission, one patient flatly refused to give his name. Not wishing to hold up the line, Nina asked him to step aside and wait for her in the dayroom. Twenty minutes later she joined him there, and casually engaged him in an informal exchange.

"By the way," she slipped in, "my name is Nina Brandt. What's yours?"

Without a moment's hesitation he said, "James Donham."

One G.I., insisting that God had sent him a message forbidding him to eat, refused food for five days. Nina decided he had fasted long enough. She found him sitting in his room, morose and catatonic.

"Isn't this a beautiful day!" she began. "You can see those tall trees from your window."

"Yeah," he muttered apathetically.

"Bob, I have a nice surprise for you."

"Yeah?"

"This morning I had a message from God—you know, like you've been getting."

Bob's eyes opened wide. She went on.

"Yes, God asked me to tell you he would be very pleased if you would eat something—not now, but at supper tonight."

Bob said nothing. He continued to stare. But there was no further trouble with his eating.

On her days off Nina would drop by my apartment, help me cook, listen to me practice, and run Ilsa. I soon discovered that my new friend was enormously versatile. She could cook for twenty as nonchalantly as for two, and still be ready to sit down serenely with her guests. She organized things automatically. She attributed her success with flowers and plants to talking to them. She was a mechanical wizard. Plumbing, wiring, tape recorders, movie projectors, clocks, vacuum cleaners—she could repair anything. Until the problem was solved and the mechanism worked perfectly, she was lost to the world. She had a power of describing things —a ship, a machine, a sunset—that made me see them.

Of death she said, "I don't care what happens to my body; that's only the box the gift came in."

She shrugged off her own aches and pains with a mind-over-matter attitude. Early in her Army career she suffered an injured disc from lifting a patient. The doctors wanted to operate, but Nina said, "Not on your life. Nobody's cutting into my spine." She never missed a day's work.

During the time that our acquaintance was ripening into friendship, her attitude toward life contrasted miserably with my own. I was deeper and deeper in the throes of anxiety about my future. The diplomas, degrees, concerts, broadcasts—everything seemed to end in a blind alley. Getting repeated rebuffs after all the training, yet seeing friends move easily into professional positions, reinforced my dismal sense of inadequacy.

Why? What was wrong? It must be that I just wasn't good enough. Mother had been sure everything would be fine when I grew up; she was wrong. Rudy had encouraged me to play professionally; I wasn't making the grade. I began to wonder why I was living. I longed for death.

"God, let me die, let me die," I moaned into my pillow at night. "I've tried; it's no use."

Only at the piano, when I could force myself to play, was there any relief. For this, I thought, I owe Rudy a lot. I sent off a note to him, hoping he might have a helpful idea. Within a week he replied:

> I know but too well what you are going through, but I cannot believe that anyone with your vitality and talent will not ultimately arrive. I am sending you Besant's translation of the Bhagavad Gita and a volume of Tagore. Try reading the Psalms once

in a while, little heretic. One of my favorites contains this passage:

> "In his favor is Life. Weeping may endure for a night, but joy cometh in the morning."

Try drawing on the divine reservoir."

Easier said than done. I could understand Rudy's faith. He had religion in his genes. Besides, he was a success. He had achieved in every department of his art: as teacher, performer, composer. The "divine reservoir," if that's what it was, had worked for him, but how could I use it?

Finding me in tears one day, Nina said in her usual calm voice, "You're trying too hard. Stop knocking on closed doors. Keep up your beautiful music. I know your opportunity will come. And by the way, have you ever tried praying?"

The idea was strange to me. It sounded too simple. I had always operated on the premise that if you wanted anything in this world, you had to get it for yourself. But thus far hard work had yielded only meager returns. I was ready to try anything. Experimentally, self-consciously, I began to cultivate the practice of daily prayer. "God," I prayed, "show me the purpose for which you sent me into this world. Help me to be of use to myself and to humanity."

I wasn't sure whom I was praying to or if anyone was listening, but somehow it had a tranquilizing effect. I decided it was a kind of self-hypnosis that calmed me enough to shake off some of the apathy and depression and get functioning again. Strangely, after that, things began to happen.

For the thousands of men returning from the Pacific,

San Francisco was the port of entry. The bar business was booming. Anyone who could bang out a popular tune and belonged to the union could make $150 a week for only a few nights' work. Half the concert pianists in town were joining. Why not get in on the bonanza?

Jean lent me the one-hundred-dollar initiation fee. After numerous calls, the union finally gave me an appointment for an audition. I couldn't help wondering if they also auditioned the nonclassical pianists. Jean's comment: "I hate to think of you playing for those slobs."

I giggled inwardly on the way to the interview.

"What kind of stuff do you play?" my auditioner wanted to know.

"Oh, things from the musicals and—"

"O.K., give us a sample." He sounded bored and skeptical.

After "Smoke Gets in Your Eyes" and "I've Got Rhythm," he dismissed me with "O.K., I'll call you."

I interpreted this as a smashing success—at least he hadn't mentioned the blindness business.

I played the gamut—everything from dives like the Silver Dollar, Cork and Bottle, Drift Inn, and Lonestar Bar to the posh Club Fortune in Reno. Servicemen would tip me five dollars to hear a favorite tune and often insisted on buying me a drink. Having a limited capacity, but not daring to turn away business, I primed each bartender to put a drop of the hard stuff in a glass of water. In almost every bar, a has-been or a would-be performer would sidle up to the microphone and crackle out a bourbon-flavored solo.

It was during the nightclub circuit that I donned a new piece of apparel: dark glasses. At first I hated the idea. I had grown up hearing Dorothy Parker's "Men never make passes at girls who wear glasses," but now, Nina informed me, it was very Hollywood. "Besides," she said, "they hide your only bad feature—in fact, no one would know you can't see when you have them on."

In time I got used to the goggles and was even amused when some of the drunks wanted to know, "What's the idea of the dark glasses—got a shiner or sump'n?"

The honky-tonks were boring, demeaning, and sometimes downright revolting, but they got me a fur coat and a Steinway grand!

My new occupation must forever be a secret from Rudy, I thought, for if he knew, he would write me off as a monumental failure. But after his next letter I realized he would find out.

> I have broken off my American commitments to accept a two-year tour of the China-Burma-India War theater. By pulling a few strings I can stop in San Francisco and spend a day with you. I want to rent a car and take you to Yosemite. It's a long drive, and we would have to start at dawn. I've been there before and know you will be as awed by it as I am. Can you arrange it for next Wednesday?

The idea that we were to have a whole day together at Yosemite was so astonishing and wonderful that I canceled my own commitments pronto and wired, "Marvelous! Ilsa asks if she can come, too."

[14]

Interlude at Yosemite

WHEN THE alarm went off at four thirty that morning I was already awake. I put on some coffee and excitedly showered and dressed, deciding on a bright green sweater-suit, my tan suede coat, and a flowered scarf in case it was cool in the mountains.

Hearing life stir at such an ungodly hour, Ilsa yawned, stretched, and spying me put a can of her dog food into a tote bag, shook herself alert. As usual when the bell rang, she followed me to the door. After a warm embrace, holding me away from him, Rudy said, "You look great—good Lord, it's been ages."

I offered him coffee, but he was eager to get on the road. At the car, he held open the rear door for Ilsa to jump in.

"Quite a pup," he said, "does she ever bark?"

"Yes, at five o'clock every night—time for her supper."

I could hardly believe I was going to spend a whole day with Rudy. It was unreal, particularly since I had heard from him so spasmodically. As we started off I said, "No letters from you for ages. Sometimes you just disappear into the blue."

"When that happens, I'm either out of town filling engagements or in one of those gloomy moods that descend on me occasionally. I wouldn't want to share them with anyone."

"But that's when you should write. Are you still doing your yoga exercises?"

He told me he stood on his head every day, lived mainly on vegetables and fruit juices, and fasted one day a week.

"You must be as skinny as a rail." I reached over and touched his rib cage.

"Yes, but as wiry as a monkey—those foghorns sound like the moan of ages."

"I know. The first time I heard them they scared me out of my skin. But now they're just part of San Francisco, and I love them."

"Don't you miss New York?"

"Only the theater. I could never live there again. Somehow I feel more like a person here—there's more room to breathe."

"You mean that out here they don't sell their souls for status symbols and synthetic pleasure?"

"Oh, I suppose they do, but it's so much easier to get outdoors to refuel your batteries."

"How did your radio show turn out?"

I was apprehensive of how he would feel about one of his students winding up in the honky-tonks. I told him how I thought Ilsa had mesmerized N.B.C.'s pro-

Interlude at Yosemite

gram director into giving me a spot, how I'd had to include popular fare to increase fan mail, and how finally the war had brought it all to an end.

"And now?" he asked.

Here it was. I had to confess I was playing in dives.

"Ye Gods! How do you stand it?"

"Like everything else, you get used to it. Actually, Rudy, I think it's a good experience. When the establishment uses singers, I have to transpose tunes on the spot. Always there are all sorts of requests, even for classics sometimes. Anyhow, it's worth slumming to have a bit of cash around. At the moment I have no choice."

"But you must come up against some questionable characters."

"I do indeed. But you learn to handle them. I just put my mind in neutral, and when the drunks offer to take me home I tell them my husband is going to pick me up. That stops them."

"Well, you're fortunate to be able to play by ear. I haven't done it since the old days when I played for silent movies."

"Well then, you had a taste of it too."

He laughed and rolled down the window.

"What a beautiful sky ahead," he said. "The sun is just rising and the color is gorgeous aquamarine brushed with rose and yellow—a painter's sky. It's a good omen. I believe I wrote you," he went on, "that I broke my contract with Columbia? I was invited to go on the China-Burma-India tour."

"Yes, but isn't that risky? Won't it be tough when you get back—about getting bookings, I mean?"

"I hope not. I had to take the chance. The Far East has a strange fascination for me."

He said that he would be gone two years, that he was disappointed not to be able to see Gandhi because he was confined in the Aga Khan Palace but that he had become interested in Ramakrishna, "another great Indian saint I think you'll be hearing a lot about before the end of the century. If our schedule permits I'm going to try to track him down."

He was obviously being caught up more and more in a way I thought might harm his career. His breach of contract with Columbia might have drastic consequences: He could be blacklisted.

"Well," I ventured, "don't let all that high-flown idealism take you too far out of this world."

"What's so commendable about this world?" he asked, a bit sharply.

"Granted—but life has a way, you know, of expecting us to be practical sometimes."

"Speaking of which," he said in a lighter tone, "I see a diner over on the right where a lot of trucks are parked. Truck-drivers always know the good eating places. Let's try it. You must be starved."

At breakfast, answering his questions about what I did for fun, I told him about my Sunday hikes with the Sierra Club and ice-skating and skiing with Jean and Frank.

"How in the world do you ski?" he asked.

"Well, Frank just points me in the right direction and checks carefully on my stance. After that, it's a matter of balance and strong legs. The kick turns take me back to my ballet lessons."

"Well," said Rudy, "you'll have to come out on the slopes with me some day."

Interlude at Yosemite

"Heavens, no. I'll never be that good. In fact, I think skiing is an awful lot of trouble just to slide down a hill. I can think of lots of easier ways to get a thrill."

Always as thorough and methodical in preparing for a trip as for a recital, he had looked up everything about Yosemite, its glacial origins, its establishment as a national park through John Muir. He remembered its spectacular vistas.

When we reached the foothills of the Sierra, he stopped the car and drew on my palm the contour of the U-shaped valley, indicating with his fingers the positions of El Capitan, North Dome, Cathedral Spires, the Three Brothers, and towering over all, Half Dome.

As we entered the steep, narrow gorge leading to the valley, the rock walls on either side made the motor and our voices sound muffled. Rudy suggested that we get out so I could touch the sheer rock face and sense its enormous height. Both of us simultaneously drew in a breath of sharp, pine-laden air.

"No one ever takes a deep breath in the city," he commented.

We lunched at the Lodge cafeteria, taking our trays outdoors to enjoy the nearby Yosemite Falls.

"Their total plunge," said Rudy, "is two thousand four hundred and twenty-five feet, almost half a mile. We're in luck—May is the best time to hear them, when the snows are melting fast."

Although we were the equivalent of several blocks away, we could hear their roar and feel with our feet their vibration in the surrounding earth. Birds perched in the bushes and trees around us, waiting for crumbs. The red-breasted grosbeaks were particularly brave, coming right up to us, while the blue jays, robins, and sparrows hovered a little distance away.

"You'll write, won't you," I asked, "from those exotic places you're going to?"

"I plan to keep a journal and send copies of it around to the family and friends. Hope you won't mind a carbon."

"Not at all. By the way, I love your idea of putting the stamp on diagonally to let me know the letter is from you."

"I should learn Braille. Perhaps I shall some time."

He wanted a picture of Ilsa and me in action so, at the foot of a trail, I buckled on her harness and we started up, Rudy following, camera in hand. For the next forty minutes Ilsa's brisk pace had me panting. I was very glad for the leverage of the harness, particularly over the almost perpendicular places and around tricky turns. Just before the top, Rudy called out, "Hold it!" and caught me, I suspect, in a half-crouched, froglike position.

At the crest we turned and faced in the direction from which we had come.

"From here," Rudy explained, "we see the panorama I showed you in the car. The majesty of it is overwhelming."

"I know," I said, feeling and breathing it. "Somehow it draws you into its mystery, makes you reverent, as with great music."

Rudy quoted from John Muir: "Climb the mountains and get their good tidings. Nature's peace will flow into you as sunshine flows into trees."

We stood and listened to the ageless stillness, absorbing the beauty around us.

I turned Ilsa loose and let her range out to quench her thirst and roll in patches of snow not quite melted

Interlude at Yosemite

from the winter's pack. Rudy collected sprigs of heather, larkspur, and camphor-smelling pepperwood leaves.

"You look like a wood nymph with those flowers against your green outfit." Again I heard the camera click.

"This is one I'll take to Asia." Then, sitting down next to me: "I hope you'll give up that nightclub job soon."

"Don't worry, I will. I had to take advantage of the chance to make a little money while it lasted. You know, Rudy, I miss my lessons terribly."

"I miss them too. I know I gave you a bad time that first year—probably made you miserable."

"You did, that's true. But it was the only honest way to proceed. I'll always be grateful to you for it."

"No need for that; you've taught me many things, too."

Noticing him rise, I, too, stood and brushed the leaves and pine needles from my clothes.

"This is a hard spot to leave," he said, "but I think we'd better head back. There are other wonders I want to show you."

As we started down the trail Ilsa bounded off like a fawn coming back from time to time to be sure we were following. Arm in arm, Rudy and I half-ran, half-slid over the last part of the trail.

"When I get back from Asia we'll have to make some real climbs," he said. "Next I want you to hear another beautiful but very different waterfall."

In contrast to the plunging cataracts of the Yosemite, Bridal Veil Falls sounded like a stream dancing over pebbles. From Rudy's description, I imagined that its form was like filaments of white net tumbling into the wind.

At our next stop, the government museum, the curator gave me a hand-view of valley specimens: stuffed animals, birds, huge pinecones, and models of covered wagons and Indian tepees—*oo-mah-chas,* he called them.

We drove thirty-five miles up over winding roads to the giant sequoias. From the sound of the wind in their topmost branches I calculated their awesome height. We walked through the trunk—twenty-five feet long, Rudy informed me—of the famous Tunnel Tree.

By the time we returned to the car, darkness had fallen. Ilsa, whose biological clock never failed, greeted us with sharp barks. After we had fed her, given her another run, and put her back in the car, Rudy said, "I think this day calls for dinner at the Ahwanee. It's an impressive structure—grayed wood and stone blending with the mountains, huge windows looking out on meadow and forest."

You could feel elegance the moment you entered: soft, thick rugs, high ceilings, aromatic paneled walls, music drifting in from the dining room. Rudy showed me the enormous fireplaces, lamps, and Indian wall-hangings.

Halfway through dinner, he excused himself to speak to the orchestra leader. When he returned to the table, I heard the strains of "Lovely to Look At" from "Roberta."

"That's for us," Rudy said.

His dancing was precise and conservative, but it would have been bliss even if he had stepped on my toes. The whole day had had a kind of magic quality. I wanted it never to end.

We started home under a starry sky, talking only intermittently. On the car radio, Rudy stumbled on *The Afternoon of a Faun.*

"What luck!" he exclaimed. "If I were asked to name my favorite piece in all the world, it would be this. Can you imagine that when it was first performed in 1894 in England, the audience walked out? Almost as bad as the fuss they made at the *Sacre.* Yet what two pieces have had more influence on modern music?"

We reveled in the tonal and harmonic color, the sensuous themes, the mystical instrumentation, the tranquil mood.

"It's been a perfect day, Rudy. I'll always remember it." He reached for my hand and drew me closer to him.

"You sound as though you thought it would be our last together."

"One never knows. You're going so far away."

"Hearing this music," he said, "reminds me of something I read the other day. There's a primitive tribe somewhere in Africa that believes every atom of our bodies vibrates at a certain frequency, and that each soul has its own melody. Do you suppose our souls harmonize?"

"An intriguing idea. I wonder. With your melody in the other world and mine in this, we might make lively counterpoint."

"We should select the century for at least the general style. Which would you prefer?"

"I think the nineteenth."

"You see, you're a little romantic yourself."

"But with you going away, we'll never find out."

"We'll find out, don't worry."

It was after midnight when we reached my apartment.

Ilsa sleepily ambled to her usual place by the side of the bed. Rudy looked at his watch.

"Good heavens, I'll have to rush to return the car and make my plane."

I felt a stab of disappointment. I had hoped to postpone our parting a little longer. Tossing my coat and bag on a chair, I turned to him.

"Rudy, I want to thank you with all my heart for this wonderful day, and for the pains you took to make me see that incredible valley."

"Don't thank me, dear," he answered. "You made me see it with fresh eyes."

Then, drawing me to him: "I must leave now."

I felt his lips on mine, strong, lingering. A shiver of excitement ran through me. Finally he stood back, and I felt him looking at me.

"I'll have the itinerary in a week. Write me, won't you?"

"Of course."

When the door closed, I leaned against it, listening to his footsteps receding in the hallway. The only other sound was the ticking of the Braille clock in the kitchen. I walked to the sofa and sat down.

All day I had felt an undercurrent of attraction between us—some new element of mutual involvement that made everything we experienced vivid and meaningful. I had been deeply touched by his thoughtfulness, his eagerness to share with me his love of outdoors. The difference between our temperaments—he tending to withdraw from life, me happiest in the thick of things—created no conflict. On the contrary, with my leaning toward agnosticism, I was fascinated by his faithfulness to the Christian ideal of divinity and exploration of a more mystical compass in life.

But why was I letting myself drift into such thoughts? There could never be a close relationship between Rudy and me. How could I compete with the glamorous women who flocked around him, women who could speak to him with their eyes? He would return from Asia, and a continent would separate us again. I told myself, "Don't be a fool. Come out of the clouds."

Luckily, life had helped me develop insulation, as in the old ballet class where I learned to fall without hurting myself, or like some Orientals who turn off their nerve endings when walking on hot coals.

But I was only partially successful, for that night my dreams took me back to cascading water, rock walls, aromatic wood, meadows, and music—and in the midst of it all, Rudy and I reaching toward each other with only our fingertips touching.

[15]

On Tour

MR. AND MRS. COWLER, directors of the National Transcribers Society for the Blind, rescued me from the dens of iniquity. Devout Seventh Day Adventists, they had hit upon the idea of raising funds by giving school and club programs to provide employment and "salvation" for the blind. They used the voluntary contributions from students and service groups to pay the blind for transcribing books, most of them religious, into Braille.

In the summer of 1943, they asked me to replace a xylophonist on their shows. They explained that their tours ran from October to June, that they would like me to travel with them for at least three years, that the territory covered from the West Coast to Missouri, and that the pay would be $150 a week plus all expenses. Quite an improvement over the bistro circuit! I accepted without hesitation.

Besides the Cowlers, Ilsa, and me, the troop included Velma Black, a pleasant, partially sighted woman whom the Cowlers had converted to their religion. Velma demonstrated Braille and I played two groups—one classical, the other popular—with a talk about Ilsa in between. The Cowlers took turns in introducing the program and making appeals for donations.

Mr. Cowler's first introduction struck me so funny I could hardly go on. He said, with great solemnity, "You know the blind are wonderful! The only trouble with them is they can't see."

Sometimes the student body president made the introduction. One of them was confused about the billing: "We have a good program so I hope you will all pay attention. Someone is going to talk and I understand there's a dog that plays the piano."

The students were a marvelous audience: quiet during my opening group of classics; quick to catch a mild joke in my talk; whistling, stamping, and clamoring for more of the arrangements of popular tunes and improvisations.

Of course, Ilsa was the hit on the show. To dramatize her entrance, I generally left her backstage with Velma until the end of my first group of pieces. Then I announced, "And now I want you to meet someone special. Ilsa, come." Whereupon Velma would release her and she would fly to my side, dragging her leash. I then demonstrated her obedience, described her training, and when time allowed, answered student questions.

On one program before I gave the command, "Fetch!"

she enchanted the audience by bringing me a sticky scrap of paper left on the stage floor.

Another time, Ilsa was tied to a fire-extinguisher during my opening section. When I slapped my side and called, "Ilsa, come," she bounded onstage bringing with her the extinguishing apparatus, accompanied by a loud hissing of escaping foam. The students roared and applauded wildly.

Throughout the tour, Velma and I shared a room. An easy-going person with a keen sense of humor, she helped to make the tour bearable.

Terrible things were always happening to my hose on those trips—one fell down right on stage. They were continually popping runs from the splintery piano seats. Once I developed a hole where it couldn't be seen.

"Why don't you darn it?" Velma asked.

I confessed. "You kidding? I don't even know how to thread a needle."

She tried to hide her amazement.

"Well, teach me—I dare you," I said.

So she presented me with a self-threader and proceeded to show me how to darn.

"Doesn't seem too hard," I commented optimistically.

I sewed and sewed and sewed and sewed, and when I thought my handiwork was ready for inspection, I said, "O.K., take a look. I think I've got it."

Velma looked, and, behold, there as large as ever was the hole.

"I give up," I said. "How can anybody be so stupid!" She couldn't believe it and I couldn't believe it, but the hole was there.

After that, I just quietly slipped my torn stockings into the wastebasket.

On Tour

Our schedule was grueling: four school assemblies a day, with club programs sandwiched in over the noon hour, and sometimes the dinner hour, too. The secret of survival was to sleep in the car between dates, if only for ten minutes. It didn't take long to understand why anyone who had ever played on the road said there was nothing like it to make a trooper out of you—the show went on regardless of the condition of the weather, the instrument, or your health.

In southern California we discovered that acres of orange groves with ripe fruit on the trees were a sure indication we could get only canned juice in the local restaurants. In the South and Southwest we grew tired of hominy grits and black-eyed peas, hard water, malodorous restrooms at gas stations, twanging cowboy music, people sending us "thataway" in the wrong direction.

In a Texas town Mr. Cowler rushed backstage before the program to inform Velma and me of the school seating-plan. "The Negro students are on one side of the auditorium, the whites on the other. Center aisle is the Mason-Dixon line," he whispered. It threw a pall over our entire stay in that town.

At Santa Cruz, California, I was about to begin with the fortissimo chords of the *Warsaw* Concerto. When my fingers dropped on the keys, nothing came out—not a sound. Nonplussed, I arose and asked, "Is there another piano in the house?"

A teacher rushed to the platform. "Oh, you must forgive us, Miss Resnick. We turn off the keys every lunchtime because the boys pound on them so." She pushed or pulled something, and the keys came back to life.

In Wichita, Kansas, I had the thrill of flying a Beechcraft Bonanza. After a walkaround inspection of the propeller, fuselage, wings, and tail, the pilot showed me the numerous gauges—fuel, temperature, speed, horizon, direction, a million of them it seemed—but most important, the stick that regulated descent (forward), ascent (backward), up, down, turns, and banks.

He took the plane up to twelve thousand feet and then said, "O.K., it's all yours. Let's change places."

I took hold of the stick. "What do I do?"

"Nothing till I tell you."

The plane seemed to know its destination. Only occasionally did my instructor direct me to move the stick. We cruised for forty-five minutes. Then Vic said, "Let's start down." I pushed forward on the stick and felt a sudden violent motion. "Not that much," he said, "the slightest pressure is all you need."

A mystical and thrilling experience! I hated to hand back the controls for him to land.

In March 1944, our schedule took us to Muskogee, Oklahoma, a few weeks after a devastating twister had demolished homes, flattened cars, cut power lines, toppled trees, and actually picked up people and hurled them miles away. Mr. Cowler stopped to show Velma and me the débris: window frames, plaster, splintered bric-a-brac, shredded clothing. Water still came up to the hubcaps of our car. The School for the Blind which we had hoped to visit had collapsed, killing several of the students. At a roadside stall where we stopped for a snack, we commiserated with the attendant. "You'll be moving away from here, won't you? They say you never know when these catastrophes are going to strike."

"Oh no," she said nonchalantly, "we just live through

these things somehow or other. How do you folks put up with all those earthquakes in California?"

I was to find out. In Carpenteria, a few miles south of Santa Barbara, I was about to give my talk about Ilsa when everything in the auditorium, including the piano, began to shake violently. I had never been in an earthquake before. My knees and stomach quivered as I reached for the piano to steady myself.

Happily the principal kept a cool head. From the back of the room he called out, "Everyone stay right where you are. Go right ahead, Miss Resnick."

"You don't mind if I locate the piano bench again?" I asked. "Just in case." With my knees still shaking, I finished the talk.

The days were so full, so demanding, that I rarely thought of Rudy, or of anyone at home, for that matter. Work claimed every waking moment and when my head touched the pillow I fell almost instantly into total oblivion. Copies of his travel journal arrived every few months. They told of concerts in India played in drenching rain with the audiences sitting through the entire performance; of programs in the thickest of jungles where black flies took over, so thick that "every fraction of a second either hand is not playing, it has to be used to brush the flies off my face, my hair, the music, or the keys." They told of living in an ocean of dust in Burma where you could see, taste, smell, and feel it; of a plane ride in a C47 of which the door had been shot off. "I stood right in the doorway," he wrote, "holding onto a rail at the side. Never have I had such a feeling of being merged with the Infinite. It was a terrifying but spiritually rewarding experience."

He had climbed in the Himalayas and seen the Taj

Mahal. I treasured the scribbled line at the end of one of his letters: "I think often of our beautiful day at Yosemite." It was signed, "Yours, with closest thoughts, Rudy."

After a program at a school in Oklahoma, a teacher was shaking my hand and thanking me for the music when, to my horror, Ilsa lunged at her. It was not merely a nip—it was a serious bite. As Ilsa had grown older, her protective instinct had become an increasing problem. Back at Morristown a knock on the door had brought sharp barks. She resented children, the doorbell, and deliverymen. She was so good in other ways, however—quiet, healthy, an excellent guide—that I put off doing anything about it. But this was the end. I decided to find her a place to live out her years.

By a stroke of luck, we found a bachelor whose home I wouldn't have minded sharing myself. He had a dog he said needed company, and he lived near large meadows, woods, and a river, so it was a happy arrangement for all concerned.

Although Mrs. Cowler grumbled about the loss to the program, she agreed it should be done. Anyhow, the tour would finish in only a few more months.

Mr. Cowler was patient and kind, but his wife was cranky and ill-tempered most of the time. To the school personnel she was obsequious, expressing admiration for the accomplishments of blind people. But in the privacy of our motel, she was truculent and mean.

Concerned about her weight but even more about spending money, Mrs. Cowler always scoured the town for the cheapest restaurants and motels. Gas-rationing didn't help her disposition. "I can't drive around mailing your letters," she complained. "You know we have to save gas." Yet she would drive five miles out of the way for a piece of pie or a chocolate bar she craved.

During the war years the students had money and were quite generous. Even in the poorer schools, where the usual donation was 10¢, the take averaged $50 per school, so that with four or five shows, even on slim days collections ran $250 and up per day. All of us helped separate, count, and wrap into respective rolls for bank deposits along the way the piles of pennies, nickels, dimes, quarters, half dollars, and dollars contributed by the students of each school.

When the Cowlers first described their work to me, it seemed laudable enough. What was more important than helping blind people earn a living? I had immediately signed up for three seasons. But when I learned that there were only twelve people on the payroll, I knew their motives were less than altruistic. Besides, with Braille printing presses maintained by the government and hundreds of certified sighted volunteer transcribers, this drummed-up kind of employment made no sense. The operation reminded me in many ways of Blindcraft. Instead of some thirty people making brooms, a handful punched out Braille. As with Blindcraft, the Society had no board of directors, yet the public thought it was doing great good.

By using blind people on their programs, the Cowlers were involving Velma and me in their misrepresentation. True, they were helping me earn a living, but under the circumstances it became increasingly abhorrent.

Nevertheless, the tour had been of tremendous practical value. It had restored my self-confidence and suggested new and lucrative ways of using my music. With expenses paid, and $150 a week, I had money in the bank. However, the exploitation of blind people in general, and Mrs. Cowler's disposition in particular, were too offensive for me to accept their invitation to travel with them in 1946. I returned to my apartment in San Francisco, little realizing that it would not be long before I would be on the road again.

[16]

A New Direction

Sometimes when you look back over your life, experiences that seemed haphazard and transitory as they occurred, fall into place like pieces of a jigsaw puzzle. My education with seeing children, the summers at Mossyledge, the lessons in drama and dance, my music, the stint at teaching, the exposure to social agencies, and most recently, playing and speaking in public—all these seemed isolated episodes, events that flowed past me without any connection. Now, in retrospect, I see how everything I had learned and experienced up to this time had meaning and how, as the next few years would show, practical value in a totally new avenue of my life's work.

In the summer of 1942 I was asked to speak at a meeting of the San Francisco Downtown Lions Club. Knowing that their primary interest was work for the blind,

I described the opportunities I had had as a child in New York, contrasting them with the meager services available for them locally: welfare and the Blindcraft broom shop. I said I thought San Francisco ought to have a Lighthouse, a place where blind children could run free and where adults could be trained for jobs and pursue hobbies they could share with seeing people.

The next day Dr. Walter Straub, chairman of the Sight-Saving Committee, telephoned to say that his club had been casting about for a worthwhile project and was interested in the idea, but that before investing time and money in it, the club would like me to schedule several activities to test the responses of those who would be using the center.

Between July and November of that year I arranged for a Red Cross course in first aid, a picnic in a eucalyptus grove, and a Halloween party. All who attended were welfare clients, most of them shut-ins in their mid-forties or older, some partially sighted, most totally blind. They obviously relished a chance to get out of their homes, get a breath of fresh air, and make new friends.

I committed a faux pas at the Halloween party. After ducking for apples, pinning the tail on the donkey, and swapping ghost stories, we lined the guests up in teams for relay races. For the three-legged race we paired them off, tying together the inside legs of each pair. In the process of wrapping the cloth around one pair, I jumped back in horror—one leg was wooden.

"I beg your pardon," I muttered.

But the owner was only amused. "Oh, that's O.K., go right ahead," she said.

So I tied the one good leg to the wooden one—and their team won.

A New Direction

By now the Lions were convinced that the project was needed and wanted. They incorporated the San Francisco Center for the Blind, rented a store for activities, and hired a director. At first they allowed the blind to be dues-paying members with a representative on the board of directors, but the arrangement was short-lived. At the end of the first year, the participants were so unhappy with the director that they demanded his removal. The Lions regarded this as an encroachment on their authority and terminated the group's membership privileges. From then on, dissension and complaints were to plague the center for the duration of its history.

After organizing the initial activities, I left the city for the three-year tour with the Cowlers. By the time I returned, the Lions had purchased a building with classrooms, auditorium, large dining room, and kitchen, and had the benefit of instructors paid by Adult Education. I could hardly wait to visit the center.

I arrived unannounced at about two o'clock one afternoon and dropped in first at the sculpture class. Immediately four old friends greeted me, some of the picnickers who had attended the outing four years earlier. They introduced their instructor and showed me samples of clay ashtrays, bowls, and figurines they had made. Impressed, I asked the instructor if he had ever taught modeling to the blind before.

"No," he said, "but touch is what it's all about, so it has never been difficult. I start by having them sculpt their own hands; then, from models, they make objects and animal figures, and some day they'll do human figures. These people are talented. In fact, we're planning to show a number of pieces in the city exhibit next month."

I next drifted into the smoke-filled lounge. I heard card shuffling from a table in the middle of the room, a baseball game coming out of a radio, and a man and two women chatting on a couch.

"Rose! Goodta see ya, where ya been? Sit down. Gosh, it's been ages." I recognized the rasping voice of old Schwartz, another of the picnickers. He had left his card game and joined us by the couch.

"How are things going?" I asked.

"Terrible," two of them chorused.

"This place is like a morgue," said Wanda, a middle-aged woman whom I remembered as short and obese.

"We've had a lot of trouble," Schwartz went on, "we complain but nobody listens to us. Didja hear? We ain't got no say in the runnin' of this joint. There's been four directors since you left."

"Yeah," chimed in Butcher, the young-sounding man on the couch, "and the one we've got now distributed food in Europe during the war. He was a food salesman before that. What does he know about runnin' an agency like this?"

"But you have several classes. The people in sculpture like it very much."

"Yeah, but these things they give ya around here won't help get off welfare," complained Butcher. "I need a job."

"Who needs Braille?" This from the second woman on the couch. "I'd rather listen to a Talking Book. The best thing they've got around here is lunches."

"Yeah," countered Schwartz, "and you wouldn't come for them either if they didn't pick ya up and cart ya home in a station wagon."

A New Direction

"How about weekends?" I wanted to know. "Any outings or trips?"

"You kiddin'?" It was Butcher again. "They collect us at ten o'clock and take us home at two thirty. That's it, sister. This place is closed tighter'n a drum evenings and weekends."

"Have any of you tried talking with the director?"

"That don't do no good," declared Wanda. "Pence says we're going to have monthly dances. I can imagine what they'll be like. A bunch of blinks dancin' with each other."

"Well," I offered, "perhaps I can talk to him."

"Aw, he treats all blinks the same," Schwartz groaned, "and he won't treat you any different. He's sorry for us. He doesn't think we're as good as he is."

Obviously, the breach between the clients and the director, as well as the board, had been complete. Without an official means of communication, they could only complain among themselves. The door to the outside world had snapped shut and trapped them inside. And, as at Blindcraft, there were no leaders, no one articulate or confident enough to protest on their behalf. Dreariness, stagnation, and a sense of futility had grown and festered among them.

If Mrs. Quist had been listening, she would have expressed her usual reaction to such ventilation. "Grady, the blind are such an ungrateful lot." And, in a sense, these people were. The Lions had provided a building and paid for operating expenses, maintenance, drivers, and a director. Their intentions had been the best. The center at least took a number of shut-ins out of their homes each day, exposed them to new learning experiences, and afforded them an opportunity to meet people with whom they shared a common problem.

Yet I knew that no programming could compensate for the withdrawal of the right to speak for themselves, and for what they felt to be a condescending attitude on the part of the administration. The Lions had selected a businessman with a food background to do a job that required related training, experience, and at least some understanding of the psychological and social implications of blindness.

Pence had an office only a few steps down the hall. Quietly pushing open the door, I asked, "May I speak to you for a few minutes?"

"Come in, come in," he said in a loud voice. "I'm always pretty busy, but what is it?"

"Oh, I was just wondering how things are going—we haven't met." I started to introduce myself, but he broke in.

"Yes, I know who you are. The Lions have mentioned you. I heard you were here. One of the girls said you were visiting. Aren't those great ashtrays they're making? Well, we're just comin' along fine. Hard for these old folks to get the Braille. Dull sense of touch, don't you know. But they do love to play cards and we have great lunches. Have you heard about our birthday dinners?"

"No, they mentioned the good lunches."

"Yes, we have wonderful lunches, and we're starting birthday dinners once a month—to celebrate birthdays falling in that month, you know. We'll have a cake, get it donated, you know, and maybe bring in a little entertainment for the folks. Social time, don't you know. Our folks don't get much in the way of a good time."

He had risen and was obviously edging me out the door.

A New Direction

"Come back and have lunch with us some time. Wish I had more time."

I noticed that his breathing was staccato and that he gave a frequent gurrumph to relieve postnasal congestion.

He impressed me as nervous and pompous. I understood the clients' feelings about his patronizing manner. They were quite right about his attitude toward blind people—he thought of them as "folks," the same in temperament, interest, needs. He could think of them only in terms of their handicaps, not as people. Confronted with probably the first blind people he had ever known, he regarded the purpose of the center as a place to help them pass the time of day, divert them with busywork, and serve them a tasty lunch. It was a travesty of what I had envisioned as a Lighthouse in the West.

Having been away three years and heard nothing during that time from the Lions, I wondered just how much help I could be. I decided to call Dr. Straub, the man to whom I had first outlined the project. Perhaps he would be amenable to meeting with some of the center clients to learn firsthand how they felt. But on the phone it was as if I were a stranger.

"I visited the center the other day," I began. "You Lions are to be congratulated for that fine facility."

"Yes, we've come a long way. Mr. Pence is doing a fine job."

"Have you ever met with any of the center people?" I ventured.

"Well, we've been out there and watched, but we don't like to interfere."

"I mean, you don't plan any meetings with them to hear how things are really going?"

"Oh no. That's up to Mr. Pence. We certainly

wouldn't interfere with him. He's a very capable man, and loves those people."

I could see I was getting nowhere. Obviously he regarded the call as interference, but I thought I ought to mention the need for a youth program.

"I was wondering if the Lions would like to add a department for children. You know, there is nothing for them in this area other than the School for the Blind."

"No, I don't think we care to take on anything more than we have now. We're very happy with our program as it is."

The message was clear. The center no longer needed me. But as though to confirm my conviction of the need for a program for blind children, a mother at a Parent-Teachers Association meeting asked, "Is there any recreation for visually handicapped children? My daughter is losing her sight. She used to play with the children on the block, but now she stays in her room after school. She's becoming depressed and withdrawn. What should I do?"

"As far as I know," I said, "there really aren't any recreational opportunities for blind children. You do take her with you on family outings, don't you?"

"Yes, but she doesn't like to come with us. We don't know how to get her over this. Another problem is that my husband is gone, I have to work, and her older sister —the only other member of our family—is entering her teens and is too engrossed with her own fun to help Linda."

"If you'll give me your name and address," I promised, "I'll get in touch with you. I've wanted to do something about this for a long time."

I wrote to Washington, Sacramento, and Los Angeles

A New Direction

to ask if there were any programs in California for blind children other than a residential school. Los Angeles had special classes for the blind in public schools—that was all. Constructive services for blind children were definitely needed. But how would I go about it? Where would I start?

It so happened that at this time Nina and I were at the crossroads of our lives. I had bid goodbye to the Cowlers, and she was on terminal leave from the Army Nurse Corps. To what would we now turn our energies?

Seated on pillows before a crackling fire in our apartment (Nina had moved in with me to get away from the Army), we talked it out. The middle of the night is a big, wide time for talk. Cars, phones, and people are still. The air is quiet, clear. Time sheds the compulsions of the day. Thought moves nimbly, gathering up chunks of the past, trying to draw from them portents of the future. Although I had been on the road most of the time since we had met, Nina and I had become good friends. We shared a love of music, the outdoors, books, the theater. We reacted the same way to people. We put them all in two classes, the real and the phony, and we had neither the time nor inclination for phonies.

"Why don't we think of something we can do together?" she asked.

"Something that can go on in the world after we're no longer here," I said.

"How about starting a home for retired guide dogs?" she proposed.

I laughed. "A darling idea, but I know one that's needed more. What would you think of starting a camp for blind children?"

"But I don't know anything about camps—I've never been to one."

"Well, I do. I remember vividly everything that happened at Mossyledge. We would make the campers feel like one big family. They'd have fun and learn a lot, but they would have responsibilities—it would be a kind of preparation for living."

"Sounds intriguing, but what would happen to your music? You can't give that up."

"Oh, no! I don't think I could live without my music. But maybe I wouldn't have to. This might be just a hobby. We don't know; we'd have to wait and see. The problem is, how do we raise the dough?"

"Couldn't we take a leaf out of the Transcribers' book? Only this would be for something real and worthwhile. Now that I'm free and still on Army pay, I could book some programs for you."

"Oh Nina, would you?"

"Well, I don't know how good I am at agenting, but I could take a shot at it. I'd go to the same schools you played at. They'd probably be tickled to have you back. I'd tell them what you told me—how much it would mean to these kids that are shut up for most of the year—and I'll bet the students would be delighted to help something like that."

It was as though some invisible hand was subtly drawing us into a new world of interest and endeavor.

"Nina," I said, "this is getting more exciting every minute."

And so began a million-dollar project.

[17]

How Do You Build an Organization?

WITH ILSA'S replacement—a honey-blond part-shepherd, part-collie, Nina and I set out that fall to fill the bookings she had made in northern California, Oregon, and Washington. At first she was too shy to take any part in the program. Impossible, she couldn't do it. But since there frequently was no one else to do it, she eventually agreed to open and close the show. Later, by an unexpected fluke, she played a more dramatic role.

Julian Proskauer, a member of the American Society of Magicians, preceded us on one school assembly. Afterward, over coffee, he intrigued us with a novel suggestion.

"I have a wonderful idea for you two. It would be a sensational addition to your program."

Nina groaned. "Oh no—not another idea! Rose started as a pianist, next came the dog, then the nightclub agents told her she had to learn to play jazz and sing popular songs. Now you're not going to turn her into a sleight-of-hand artist, are you?"

He grinned. "Well, in a way, yes. Both of you would be involved. You two are a natural for a musical mind-reading act. It's very simple. I'll send you the code."

Mind-reading! Musical mind-reading! My first reaction was negative. Would it be right to fool an audience? But Julian insisted this was just another form of entertaining with magic. When he described the procedure, it sounded very complicated. I wasn't at all sure we could pull it off. But after we played around with the code, we couldn't resist the lark of trying it.

At meals, on drives to engagements, and in our beds at night, we rehearsed, Nina feeding me sentences with the code words and I identifying them by number. Finally, at the close of a program in Washington, thoroughly frightened, our hearts pounding, we tried it out.

Nina introduced the act.

"Today, before we leave, we have a special treat for you. Miss Resnick and I have worked so closely together that we are often able to tune in on each other's thoughts. This will require complete quiet so that Miss Resnick and I can concentrate. We're going to let you ask for any one of these one hundred pieces on this typed list. You may look quickly over the list, and indicate to me which piece you would like Miss Resnick to play. We will then concentrate and she will play your request."

Then, approaching a student who had raised his hand, Nina very softly asked him to point to a song he wished me to play. In the code Number 2 was the word "now"; Number 4, the word "concentrate."

"Now be sure to concentrate."

My fingers flew to the Brailled code at my side to find Number 24. The opening strains of "Nola" brought the house down.

"Can everyone please try not to make a sound?" asked Nina. No one had any inkling that "can" meant Number 1, and "try" Number 3—for "Stars and Stripes Forever," Number 13. It worked like a charm—the students went wild. The "psychic" act became our standard close.

In one school we had a hard time suppressing our amusement when in all earnestness a science teacher said, "We'd better get that vase off the piano. It might interfere with the thought vibrations."

A student from Spokane, Washington, sent me her clipping from the Libby *News* of November 22, 1946:

LADY ROSE AND SEEING EYE DOG GIVE STUDENTS
OUTSTANDING ENTERTAINMENT
BY LUELLA PAUL

Lady Rose, who has been blind since birth, amazed the audience by playing *Warsaw* Concerto, "Clair de Lune," "Yankee Doodle," "Around the World," and many others, but most of all by her mindreading.

"Think of a Tune—She Plays It" is how she is advertised, and how she truly is. Several students from the audience were chosen to think of a tune and the amazed looks on their faces when she played it on the piano showed us she was truly great.

By the end of 1946 the tour had raised two thousand dollars, enough to cover two weeks of camping for twenty children. Now to set up the agency, raise the money to operate it, inform the public, locate a camp, recruit the staff, and find the blind children.

How did one go about setting up an agency? Neither Nina nor I had the slightest idea, but obviously we would need an attorney. Digging around in my memory, I thought of Ernest Torres, a corporation lawyer I had met in a public-speaking class. Ernest not only agreed to write the articles of incorporation; he volunteered continuing legal services. For an accountant Torres sent us to the Department of Internal Revenue. Luck was still with us: There we found a certified public accountant willing to set up and keep the books.

In February 1947 we incorporated Recreation for the Blind as a nonprofit, tax-exempt organization. To publicize the new project we wrote press releases, arranged radio interviews, sent out public-service announcements, and printed a folder, "The First Western Camp for Blind Children." We adopted as our motto the words of a medieval philosopher: "The greatest charity you can perform is to prevent the need for charity."

Until there was enough money to rent an office, we used our apartment: banging out hundreds of appeal letters; stuffing envelopes; making calls to friends, civic groups, service clubs, businessmen, foundations. We scheduled talks for schools, colleges, medical training centers, health and welfare departments, and churches.

At this point Torres said, "The agency has to have an executive director, Rose, and I guess you're the logical one."

I discovered what that implied only by doing what had to be done. About one thing Nina and I were certain. The agency would never become institutional. We would always care about the individual, treat him with respect, believe in his worth whether he was rich or poor, old or young, staff or volunteer, black or white, sighted or blind. The clients would have a voice in the program. The agency would function as a gateway to the seeing world. It would give blind people the opportunities to develop self-confidence and skills, to explore their own potential for independent living and normal companionship. This would require public education as well as rehabilitative services. Obviously, we would have to start small. Nina and I would work without compensation until the organization had more than enough money to cover the cost of services.

My friends thought I was mad. "You've worked so hard, and waited so long for a break," they said. "How can you throw it all up for anything as tenuous as a nonprofit venture?"

"But I don't think I have to give it up," I said. "This will be just a hobby."

Rudy, now teaching again in New York, was all in favor of it.

"What a beautiful use of your music," he wrote. "That is," he cautioned, "if the project, which sounds enormous, leaves you enough time to practice."

From my observations of the Meinke, Quist, and Cowler operations, I was keenly aware of the need for a knowledgeable and interested board of directors. Some of those we approached were mystified. "You mean blind children can swim, run, and play ball?" Others commented, "A camp for blind children! Heavens, why hasn't anyone thought of it before?"

We still had much to learn about selecting directors, but we were extremely fortunate in assembling for our first board a state field-worker for the blind, an ophthalmologist, a member of the San Francisco Board of Supervisors, the Board of Education Supervisor of Physically Handicapped Children, an attorney, a judge, a businessman, and our accountant. The board minutes and funds were annually audited, first by Price Waterhouse, later by Haskins and Sels.

To learn how to run a camp, Nina and I spent a weekend with Emalita Cohen, director of Timbertall, a YWCA camp one hundred miles north of San Francisco. I felt confident about programming—I had only to remember the activities of my own camping days. But I know nothing about camp administration.

We took extensive notes on camp supplies, songs, and books on camping. Practical as always, Nina asked how we should go about finding someone to run the camp without pay.

"Nina," the director said, "you've been supervisor of a hospital ward. You could do it yourself; it's not too different."

She gasped. "Me! This is the first camp I've ever stepped into."

"That's not important," said Emalita. "Running a camp involves judgment, organizing ability, skill in selecting staff. The director supervises registration, camp sanitation, maintenance, and the kitchen, and presides at staff meetings. All that should be a breeze for you with your nurse's training and Army experience. With Rose to train the staff and to direct the program, you two should make a perfect team."

Then and there Nina became the camp director, and until several years later when the job grew too big, the camp nurse as well.

Now came the crucial matter of staff recruitment. We wanted healthy young men and women who previously had worked with youth and had skills as swimmers, craftsmen, or musicians. Through the local colleges we found them all eager and willing to help—and as volunteers. Through the board of education we found a state-licensed cook. Several Scout and Campfire-trained leaders offered to work as living-unit counselors.

There still remained the problem of a facility. Where would we find a camp unused for two weeks of the summer and within our limited means? We talked with Josephine Duveneck of the American Friends Service Committee, owner of a ranch in Los Altos, forty miles south of San Francisco.

She told us that it had been rented until the last two weeks in August.

Nina spoke up. "That would be perfect for us. It would give us time to prepare. How much would it cost?"

"Fifteen dollars for the two weeks."

Fifteen dollars! Glorious lady! We were now ready to register campers, and expecting that the School for the Blind would be a natural source of referral, visited the superintendent.

"Good idea," he commented, "except that most of these kids belong in a sanitarium."

We were shocked. What an attitude for the head of a school for the blind! But it shouldn't have surprised me because it was Dr. French—the same man who had sent me off to work for a master's degree and teaching certificate, only to summarily dismiss me when I returned with both.

Finding the campers was still more difficult than raising money or setting up the agency. Without access to a central registration of blind children, we sought assistance at the City Health Department. Realizing that the release of a list would be a breach of confidentiality, we asked the officials if they would be willing to simply inform the parents of this new free camping service for blind children. Their response: "We cannot put ourselves in the position of recommending an untried program."

This lack of cooperation and resistance to Recreation for the Blind was a thorn during the first five years of operation. It baffled its founders. Despite Nina's R.N. and her work with mentally ill as well as blinded soldiers, and despite my academic credentials and firsthand knowledge of blindness, the specialists regarded us as unprofessional, interlopers in the field of social service. They suspected our motives and called us opportunists. Was it jealousy? Could they be afraid the new agency would encroach on their territory? We came to recognize this attitude as just part of the blindness system.

"A camp for the blind," they said, "means segregation." Yet we knew that most of the blind, old or young, never stirred out of their homes for vacations geared to their needs and lacked both the means and the opportunity for outdoor pleasure. Time would bring most of them around.

Deluged with so many new responsibilities, I had forgotten the logical place to start locating blind children: the mother of the visually handicapped child who had sought my help at the P.T.A. meeting. There, at least, was one child.

"Don't worry," Mrs. Ballard assured me on the telephone, "you'll have plenty of kids. I know one mother, a Mrs. Flynn, with a girl who attends the School for the Blind in Berkeley. If she goes—and I know Mrs. Flynn will want her to—she'll certainly spread the word to her friends."

When Nina and I arrived at her small, dark flat, Barbara—the fourteen-year-old blind daughter—was doodling in the kitchen. An asthmatic sister was stooped over sewing in the tiny living room.

We explained what we had come for.

"It would be a blessing," said Mrs. Flynn, with a deep sigh. "Barbara has never been out of the city. Summers are endless around here. We have only welfare to live on and can't afford amusements or trips of any kind, even close by."

Through Barbara, through notices in the newspapers and announcements on the air, we soon had our quota of twenty campers. We ordered food and supplies, arranged for insurance and for transportation to and from the camp for the children, via Red Cross bus. A doctor volunteered free examinations two weeks prior to, and immediately after, camp opening.

We were off to a splendid start.

For most of the children, Hidden Villa was the first opportunity for outdoor fun, walking alone, running relays, gathering wood, building a fire, making their own beds, keeping their cabins clean. White and black children helped each other get to the swimming pool; shy children begged for parts to be enacted around the campfire.

One day walking down the path with Lana, a polio victim, I noticed a strange creaking sound. "Listen to the cricket," I said.

Lana laughed. "Oh no, that's just my braces clinking."

"I'm sorry, honey," I said, feeling stupid. "Forgive me."

"That's nothing," she said chuckling. "I used to be sensitive about my braces, but camp is helping me to get over all that. I used to be afraid of things, too—when I first came to camp I was scared of the water—but now that I've learned to swim, I'll never be afraid of anything in life again."

Those two weeks gave Nina and me an inkling of what camp could mean to blind children.

"We no longer say to Johnny, 'Stay here, honey, we're going in for a swim,' " wrote one mother. "We just say, 'Come along, we're going swimming!' "

"Can I come back? Can I come back next year?" This was music to our ears—an assurance of success.

To all, we said, "Of course—you'll get an invitation next spring."

But our bank account was depleted. Where would we find the funds for the next session? Again we wrote hundreds of letters, gave talks, and showed a silent film of the Hidden Villa session, this time raising enough to send thirty children to camp.

In 1948, not daring to risk the water shortage which had developed at Hidden Villa, Recreation rented Loma, a hot, dusty 4H camp in the Santa Cruz mountains, large enough to accommodate thirty children. It was very primitive—the younger children slept outdoors in war-surplus beds, the teenagers in sleeping bags on the ground. Without any building on the site, campers and staff ate outdoors, pestered by flies and bees; the latrines were long rows of wooden seats in outhouses. Nina organized "bucket brigades" to scrub, sweep, and put chemicals into the toilets every morning after breakfast. Inspectors from the forestry department said they had never seen Camp Loma look as clean or smell as sweet.

The campers, of course, felt the inconvenience less than the staff. As long as they could swim, make things to take home, have good food, and be free to play outdoors, they were happy. Nevertheless, it was obvious that Recreation must someday buy a camp of its own.

Upon our return from Loma, the office received an interesting call: "Say, you run a camp for blind kids, don't you?"

"Right."

"That's a wonderful thing. I've noticed pictures in the papers of them swimming and riding and making things. I'd like to help raise money for you. I've had a lot of experience in this sort of thing. Could I come over and talk with you about it?"

Could he! The quicker the better.

Prompt for his appointment, tall, lean, in tweeds, with a friendly manner, he rather impressed us. He hastened to explain that he had handled a very successful benefit show for a group in Richmond, California, and that he would like to arrange a similar promotion for Recreation for the Blind. We asked for references.

"Just call Mrs. Chamberlain," he said. "She's a member of the board of education here and knows me well."

Mrs. Chamberlain recommended Jerry Warren without reservation: "He's a man of ideas and tremendous drive."

Jerry not only wanted a benefit show; he wanted it at the place which would accommodate the largest audience, the Civic Auditorium. It seemed ambitious for a young agency, but when Jerry assured the board that he could line up free entertainment and fill the hall, we decided it might be just the thing to get us off the ground.

But Recreation was in for a number of shocks. After it paid $450 for the rental of the hall, the Musicians' Union informed the board they would have to pay every other expense: orchestra, electricians, curtain-pullers, stagehands, ticket-takers. Nina and I took to the telephone, the typewriter, the radio, to drum up an audience large enough to fill the hall.

Jerry had lined up a Chinese troupe, and as featured artists, Ted Lewis and Jerry Marshall, early television stars. On the night of the show, to our horror, the headliners refused to come. But Jerry took it all in stride, simply ordering more of the Chinese troupe: jugglers, acrobats, zither-players.

At about eleven o'clock we began looking at our watches. The acts kept coming and coming. The merest whisper of applause brought one after another back for encores. At eleven forty-five, to put an end to this interminable procession, we introduced the mother of one of the campers for some concluding remarks. Mrs. Swanson said, "Camp was wonderful. It meant so much to my little girl." She pointedly finished with, "Thank you all for coming."

The houselights went on and the audience finally filed out.

Two days later a note from Jerry set us back on our heels. "Enclosed you will find the bills for the show. If you don't pay them immediately, I'll sue."

Sue! Why suddenly so hostile?

We were utterly bewildered. Here was a man who had presented himself as interested only in helping blind children. He had been so friendly, so cordial. The bills added up to $3,077. The list contained unauthorized items such as a salary for his wife, posters, printing, postage, and office supplies. We promptly notified Edith Johnson, assistant district attorney and member of our advisory council. She said she would look up his record at the Hall of Justice.

Edith called back the next day. "I don't think this man will want to go to court," she said. "He has a prison record as long as your arm. But you can't use this information. Once a man has paid his debt to society, it is an offense punishable by law to divulge such information or use it against him in any way."

An ex-con! My God! How would we deal with him? Would we be safe in our apartment?

"Better answer his note," Edith advised. "Tell him we'll pay only for the items we authorized."

We checked our records for the list of authorized purchases, but even before agreeing to pay for those, we decided to verify the authenticity of the bills by asking Jerry to furnish all invoices. These we promptly received from an attorney he apparently maintained on a contingency basis. Nina had the precarious job of delivering our check and collecting Recreation's supplies. Would she be shot on arrival? To our immense relief, that errand, made to his attorney's office, was the last we ever heard or saw of our eager impresario.

And what did the "benefit" net the organization? Twenty-three dollars! A bitter but worthwhile lesson, for although it meant little in cold cash, the show catapulted the Camp for Blind Children into public awareness and made it a household word in the community.

By the end of 1948, Recreation could afford a modest

office and secretary. Remembering how much Saturdays had meant to Miss Guy's girls in the old New York Lighthouse days, we launched a year-round Saturday program. With the help of volunteers and the use of city facilities, we scheduled classes in swimming, crafts, dramatics, and dance. Sighted boys and girls from Scouts, Campfire, and Y's joined our blind children for trips to the museum, zoo, parks, playgrounds, beaches, and woods, and for bowling, skating, and tandem bicycling. A charm school contributed a course in grooming; a ski resort, ski lessons, and a weekend of fun in the snow. Describing the snow trip in her San Francisco *Chronicle* column, Marjorie Trumbull wrote:

> They couldn't see the dazzling whiteness of the snow or the contrasting green pines and vivid blue sky. They couldn't know what fascinating zigzag pattern skis make down a hillside or that their own breaths made a wisp of smoke in the crystal air, but they could hear and smell and, most of all, sense the beauty they were in, and keep it with them always."

True, but more deeply gratifying to them, I thought, were the exhilaration of vigorous, outdoor activity and the awareness that they could share a sport popular with their peers.

Since its inception, Recreation had accepted campers from all over the state. Hearing about our year-round Saturday program, the Los Angeles campers wanted to know, "How come we don't have any fun like that?"

On one of our trips to southern California, therefore, Nina and I recruited volunteers through the University of California at Los Angeles. We interested a service group called the Freelancers in financing the first year-round recreation program for blind children there. Eventually Henry Bloomfield, a member of Recreation's board, donated the property which today still serves as a camp for the blind children of southern California.

After the third session at the Boy Scout Camp Royanneh, in 1949, we were more than ever convinced that Recreation had to acquire its own property. There were bridges without railings, inadequate space for storage of supplies and equipment. The children were obliged to learn to swim in a rocky creek. Off went reams of letters describing our basic requirements: plentiful water supply, at least one substantial building, swimming pool, sunny climate, and location near medical facilities. Together we investigated every lead. Up and down the state we drove, visiting more than thirty sites, some too close to commercial resorts, others too remote from supplies. One, offered free, was in dry rattlesnake country.

Finally, in a discouraged mood, almost ready to compromise, we settled on a ranch sixty miles south of San Francisco that had no pool but seemed acceptable in other respects. No sooner had Recreation put a deposit on it, however, than a neighbor, a neurologist who used his country place as a retreat, protested bitterly.

"How can I ever get any rest with a bunch of kids running and screaming around all summer?"

"But," we pointed out, "we've already put a thousand-dollar deposit on it."

"Oh, that's simple. We'll gladly reimburse your organization every penny."

Without any hesitation, the board acceded to his wishes. Fortunate indeed it proved to be, for what we ultimately found was much larger, far more beautiful, and better in every way for the realization of our dream.

It came in a notice from Mr. Epler, a real-estate man in Napa County, an area we had not explored. "Owned by Mr. and Mrs. Griffith," the notice said, "Lokoya Boys Camp has been used as both a camp for children and a resort. It has many buildings, a pool, lake, good supply of water and excellent climate. Location, sixty miles north of San Francisco, eleven miles northwest of Napa on Mt. Veeder Road."

[18]

Where the Trees Sing

As we curved and climbed along the county road leading to the old resort camp, Nina exclaimed, "Rose, this country is gorgeous! Woods, canyons, streams, and—it's amazing, there's not another car on the road."

"Yes," said Epler, "the mobs haven't discovered this little mountain yet. Wait till you see Lokoya Camp. I don't think it could be duplicated anywhere in the state. It's ideal."

I rolled down the car window to feel the direct sun on my skin and listen to a rushing stream that joined us halfway up. At an elevation of 1,500 feet, Epler turned onto a bumpy dirt road, continued almost a mile, then said, "Here we are."

Under an arcade of olive trees we entered the Griffiths'

property. We found our guide in a palm-shaded swing on a stretch of lawn in front of the camp office—the Lodge, she called it. The air was full of that tantalizing scent of freshly cut grass and now and then a whiff of honeysuckle.

"I'm glad you both wore stout shoes," Mrs. Griffith said, rising to greet us, "because it takes quite a hike to see all of our grounds."

Before embarking on the walking tour, Nina showed me nearby trees heavy with plums and figs and the low palm whose bark, hanging shaggy and papery away from the trunk, surprised me. Mr. Epler left to talk with Mr. Griffith.

"Our place has quite a history," Mrs. Griffith said as we started off down the gravel camp road. "This upper area was a resort for years before we got it. 'Solid Comfort,' they called it. The old stagecoach used to bring people up here. It met them at Napa River. They'd come up by boat from San Francisco. The adult guests still use this ranch house."

Between a sequoia and a magnolia in full bloom, we entered a ten-room house, surrounded on three sides by a sleeping porch. It overlooked a lake—really a large pond—rimmed by oak, madrone, cypress, and willow trees and full of talkative black and white ducks. Alongside, rowboats were moored to a rickety dock.

"Now let me show you one of our favorite spots," Mrs. Griffith said, taking us off the camp road into deep woods. Through a narrow opening in the trees, we stepped into the quiet cool of the spring house, protected by shoulder-high brick walls. Cold, clear mountain water bubbled out from moss-covered rocks. I heard a soft rustle in the brush behind us, a rabbit scurrying by. Squirrels darted about in the branches. Bluejays, robins, wrens, and meadowlarks welcomed us to their sanctuary. Warm sunshine glinted through fir and redwood. Nina and I turned to each other and almost simultaneously whispered, "This is it."

"We have lots of sunshine," Mrs. Griffith went on. "We're up about fifteen hundred feet, out of the fog, you know. Do you like watercress? There's a load of it around here in the spring." She gathered some.

"And get a whiff of this," she said, handing me a clump of mint.

"Is this the only water source?" Nina wanted to know.

"Oh, no, we have abundant water. Come along. I'll show you many more springs as we look around."

Continuing down the camp road, we passed a horse corral, a large swimming pool, and the games field, finally arriving at a redwood forest, the children's area. Mrs. Griffith showed us through the large, red-doored mess hall and kitchen that stood at the head of a clearing in the trees. In front of it she pointed out a natural campfire setting, fourteen redwoods connected by logs, obviously camper seats. To the right of Redwood Circle, paths led to the girls' and boys' shelters and washrooms. Deeper into the forest we followed a narrow trail, crossed a rustic bridge, and came upon the camp chapel. Redwood logs covered a gentle slope towards the altar, a redwood stump. We stood silent and reverent, drinking in the blend of hay, moss, and Douglas fir, listening to a brook at the far right singing away under chest-high ferns. Mrs. Griffith said she could take us farther on in the property but that the rest was just forest.

We couldn't believe it. What a find! Buildings, a pool, plentiful water, woods, even a lake for boating. It had everything we needed. We *had* to have it! But how to meet the Griffiths' price, $100,000?

For sound advice we consulted Clarence Lindner, a friend of Recreation, then publisher of the San Francisco *Examiner*.

"Nothing is worth one hundred thousand dollars. Better talk to them again," he said.

By some miracle, after several conferences, the Griffiths agreed to sell Recreation 320 acres, one third of their property, for $65,000. The parcel included all the major buildings and 100 acres of wooded land.

At the time Recreation had exactly two thousand dollars in the bank. How in the world we ever had the nerve to take on the responsibility of raising the required amount, I cannot now imagine, but take it on we did. With all our other duties—mailings to annual contributors, office correspondence, club engagements, preparation for the 1950 camp season (lining up of staff; screening of camp applications; ordering of supplies; arranging for transportation, insurance, and medical examinations), maintenance of records, and writing of reports, and the usual meetings incumbent on welfare-agency personnel—we had no choice but to seek professional help. We consulted a well-known San Francisco firm, the Robling Company.

We warned them that we were apprehensive of fund-raisers, relating our ill-fated experience with Mr. Warren. They said it would cost us nothing if Recreation would pay all expenses.

The board decided to hire the Robling Company. But, as it turned out, they functioned only as advisers. We found ourselves more than ever involved in address-

Where the Trees Sing

ing envelopes, writing releases, composing special folders, digging up new sources of help.

The Robling Company raised $24,000 and casually submitted a bill for expenses amounting to $13,000. The board was aghast. The bill included salaries for each man Robling had assigned to the job. In a literal sense, he had kept his word—he got no fee—but by putting his staff on Recreation's payroll, he was ahead $10,000. Despite this maneuver, Robling had helped Recreation raise the necessary $10,000 for the down payment, and had added hundreds of names to its mailing list. Recreation signed an agreement to complete payments on the property within three years.

The next order of business was to change the name. On seeing the property, one of the Robling men had suggested "Enchanted Mountain," but since it wasn't really a mountain and since that might frighten parents, we changed it to "Enchanted Hills."

Nina and I then resorted to our usual fund-raising method, setting off on a statewide tour of service groups. Result: Lions Clubs contributed camperships, supplies, equipment, and nine redwood cabins.

The December 5, 1952, issue of the Los Angeles *Times* carried the story:

BLIND GROUP'S STEER HITS STOCK SHOW'S TOP MONEY—$3,150. AUCTIONED THIRTEEN TIMES AS BUYERS DONATED HIM BACK FOR RESALE TO AID CHILDREN'S CAMP.

From the wives of the Vernon Lions Club came a Christmas tree with a crisp dollar attached to each of its fifty branches. The Ukiah Lions' president donated his prize from a drawing, two baby lambs; the newspapers captioned the story, "Bottle Baby Goes to Camp."

From service groups around the state came the camp's most prized possession, a public-address system from the Pittsburgh Kiwanis Club. They installed a top-quality phonograph and loudspeaker in the lodge, rewired the electricity throughout the entire property, and placed loudspeakers on trees near the pool, lake, and ranch house. Appropriate music wakened us in the morning, floated out over the lake to the boatmen, and quieted the campers after taps.

Omega Nu, a rural Junior League with fourteen chapters in northern California, contributed thousands of dollars each year. Helen Rowe, one of the group, founded the Davis Auxiliary whose numerous gifts included camperships, a dishwasher, a washing machine, a station wagon, and a grand piano. When television networks were fat with giveaway shows, I appeared on *Strike It Rich* and brought back a thousand dollars and a tractor for Enchanted Hills.

Public support was phenomenal, even for those times. Nina and I decided the project was meant to be. Instead of the three years the contract allowed, Recreation paid off the Griffiths' $55,000 debt in a year and a half.

Morning, noon, and night, and sometimes in my sleep, the project obsessed and possessed me. There was eternally the need to build, grow, record, train, promote. Except when letters arrived from him, even Rudy slipped into the background.

I had written him of the acquisition of Enchanted Hills, and he had replied:

> I wept with joy at the epochal news. Your various activities sound nothing short of miraculous. You

have an inner flame, Rose, which I know will one day light the way for many who live in shadow, deprived of the precious gift of sight.

After two strenuous seasons of more than three hundred and fifty concerts, I decided to treat myself to a prolonged period of composing. I've been here for four months, and plan to stay until after the Christmas holidays. Any place on an Alpine lake is Shangri-La to me—the quintessence of elements which I most love, and superior to any other place in the world.

Spiez, Switzerland, is a small, peaceful village. From my balcony I look out over picturesque chalets, villas, manors, medieval castles, and church spires, orchards and vineyards on an emerald lake. Above rise the giants of the Alps, covered with vivid green multicolored forests, and bejeweled in eternal snows.

My days have been spent mostly in composing and practicing, playing a few concerts according to whim, interspersed with thrilling mountain climbs, memorable bicycle trips, boating, swimming, tennis, and so on. It's a paradisiacal life, and one that I doubt could be duplicated anywhere.

Marvelous! He'll probably come back, I thought, with a pocketful of brilliant manuscripts. One of these days I'll write him a really long letter. But responsibilities crowded in on me so fast, his letter lay unanswered on my desk.

Prior to camp opening in June 1950, the camp staff assembled at Enchanted Hills for a week of intensive orientation. We explained the philosophy and goals of the camp, discussed the profiles of registered campers, showed a film of our tented camps, and taught the counselors adaptations of tools, facilities, and games. We demonstrated teaching techniques: for instance, that in gesture-songs, counselors would have to show each child by touch the movements of the head or hands; in the game of pitching horseshoes, the leader would provide a sound clue by tapping the goal.

When camp opened, Nina took the helm. She supervised the kitchen and maintenance, chlorinated the pool, processed medical records, set up and supervised the infirmary, and worked closely with the staff. Nina was strict with the counselors, setting forth their duties, then checking to see that they carried them out.

My job was to plan and supervise program activities, write and place publicity, and rustle up funds for everything from feed for the horses or camperships to felling trees or getting sponsors for buildings.

It was a lucky day when, through the board of education, Recreation found Christina Stephenson, the camp cook. More than a cook, Chrissy was an adored part of the camp family. She was of medium height, round-faced, with sparse graying hair and fat all over. Her high-pitched voice always had a smile in it.

Chrissy presided over the kitchen and mess hall with an iron hand. A quick sweep out the door or terrible tongue-lashing greeted any intruder between meals unless, by special permission, that person had come to the mess hall to practice the piano. And woe to the runners who arrived late to set the tables or serve, and to the counselors who raided the refrigerator at midnight or neglected to put things back where they had found them.

Once Chrissy wreaked sweet vengeance on the counselors. When she arrived early one morning to prepare breakfast, she spied a dead mouse in the honey jar on the counter. The counselors had forgotten to replace the lid. "I'll fix them," she grunted. Without removing the mouse, she put the lid back on the jar. That night, in her tent not far from the mess hall, she stayed up later than usual to hear the results. When the counselors went again to the honey jar, wild screams came from the kitchen. Chrissy fell asleep chuckling.

There was ten minutes between the first and second calls to meals, but at the very first bell, campers swarmed to the mess-hall door to serenade their "cookie." During the meal she sometimes came out of the kitchen to serve the third helping and hear the children's rhapsodic comments. Sunday dinners were masterpieces of fried chicken or roast beef, mashed potatoes, vegetables from the camp garden, and ice cream. A camper with a birthday always had a specially baked cake decorated in appropriate theme. A diving board crowned the cake for swimmers; rowers were honored with a boat.

Upon their arrival, Chrissy was always waiting with outstretched arms to greet the campers. She followed their progress from season to season. "Did you see Johnny finding his way to his cabin all by himself?" or "Look at Janie, buttering her own bread."

Although she never missed a Sunday mass, Chrissy had a big, hot delicious breakfast ready for the campers as punctually as ever on Sunday mornings, the kitchen gleaming, the helpers at their posts. Under the dishwasher always sat her fat blond spaniel, "Goldie." Every time Chrissy tasted anything, Goldie did too.

One Sunday a doctor on Recreation's board dropped

by to deliver a gift of ice cream from a city dairy. Spying Goldie, he said, "I don't think the public health people would approve of a dog in the kitchen."

Hands on hips, eyes blazing, Chrissy pounced on him. "You're a fine one to talk. You and your girlfriend roared down this dirt road in your convertible and kicked up enough dust to choke all of us. Look at this," she said, pointing out the door to clouds of dust still flying around. "Now let me show you this place. I defy anyone to find one speck of dirt. The public health can come in here any time." Goldie never budged from her headquarters.

Chrissy was not the type to complain about personal discomfort, but on one particularly hot day, she called Nina. "I've led a clean life," she said, "but this worries me." She opened the top of her smock exposing rolls of fat and a rash under her breast.

"That's just from perspiring," Nina said. "Put some baby powder on it and try to keep it dry."

But in 1954 Chrissy did run into trouble. In the spring she was in the hospital for a gall-bladder operation. They found an enlarged heart and complications from phlebitis. In three weeks Chrissy was dead. A part of camp was gone forever.

As soon as the newspapers carried stories of the acquisition of Enchanted Hills, adults began applying to come. "Where can we older folks go for a vacation? We can never find our way around in a strange place. We sit like bumps on a log unless we know someone who can come with us, but this isn't always possible."

Recreation accepted twenty adults as a start, asking for a contribution of three dollars a day, but never denying an applicant for inability to pay. "So good to be with people who understand," they said. They loved campfire, the hobby shop, music from the trees, and Sunday picnics around the lake. At one lakeside supper a duck waddled over and plucked half a chicken from a camper's plate.

Several romances flowered and ended in marriage. Dotty, sixty-two, five foot tall, and almost totally blind, had eight children, all grown, husband dead. Al, a confirmed bachelor, sixty-four, was six foot and partially blind. First they sat at the same table at meals, then they had adjacent lounging chairs by the lake, and eventually they sought each other out for the romantic waltzes in the barn. During their second session at camp, they asked if they could be married in the camp chapel.

Torrential rain forced us to hold the ceremony in the lodge instead of the chapel. The Davis auxiliary saved the day. They brought a minister, a turkey dinner, and a wedding cake for one hundred guests.

Tense, lonely, half-alive people found new confidence and freedom. A twenty-year-old man blinded in Korea had thought life was over for him. Nina taught him to row, ride, and dance. When he first came, he was surprised to find that girls still enjoyed his company. He grew less afraid of Braille when he heard fluent readings in chapel. John went home determined to lead a full life. He completed six years of preparation for social work. Today, happily married, he is on the staff of a California county welfare department.

One of the most fascinating of all our campers was Jill Russett, a deaf-blind resident of Napa. She was twenty-eight, with a beautiful figure, fine features, clear eyes, and long copper-colored hair. She "listened" in the manner of Helen Keller, placing her fingers on the speaker's lips and—to feel the vibrations—her thumb on his throat. She had spent all the years since high school "reading and feeling depressed, with no apparent reason for living," she told us.

But when Jill came to camp, we discovered that she could swim, ride horseback, and dance. She knew the shallow from the deep end of the pool by the slope of the pool floor. To find the exit, she took note of its direction from the pool filter. She could dance in perfect rhythm by first placing her hand on the jukebox and sensing the beat of the music. She was the comics editor of the camp's *Redwood Bark*.

Sue, our waterfront director, became great friends with Jill and was a frequent visitor at the Russett home. She learned to converse with Jill easily, signing into her palm. Eventually, Sue enabled Jill to go to college. Graduating cum laude from the College of the Pacific, she went on with Sue to receive a master's degree in social welfare from the University of California. Today both work as home teacher-counselors for the state.

Now that we owned the property, we were faced with the responsibility of finding a caretaker who would see that it was protected the year round. Nina's brother, Herb, had worked for a Boy Scout camp near San Francisco and was thoroughly familiar with camp maintenance and program. He had been earning a mere $150 a month, so we lured him with an additional $50 to work as a caretaker when camp was not in session and as an all-around counselor during the summer months.

Tall, blond, irrepressibly witty, and innately kind, Herb was adored by campers and staff. Wherever we needed help—and we needed it in every direction—he was right there. You might find him refereeing a ball game, teaching a group of children to swim, taking some boys on an overnight hike, clearing blackberry brambles from the areas in front of the lake or pool, or repairing the septic tank, toilets, and showers.

Herb had done a three-year stint in the Marine Corps in World War II, an experience that supplied him with stories, real and fabricated, about how many boats he had torpedoed, hardships he had breezed through, buddies he had saved, dangers he had escaped. Wherever he was, there were laughter and gaiety. He was like Harvey, who would invite a stranger on the telephone to "come on over and have a drink."

One Sunday he took a small group of Catholic campers to church in town; we expected them back immediately after mass, but Herb and his brood needed, as he put it, "A bit of after-mass fun." They had casually stopped for Cokes and then taken a detour to see the effects of volcanic action in the area. When, the following Sunday, Nina asked how many campers would like to attend services, twice as many hands went up.

Every woman in the adult session, old or young, was sure she was Herb's own true love. He waited on them, teased, flattered, cheered, consoled, and really helped them. Although we had many outstanding counselors, we never found another to match Herb. It was a blow when he left to get married.

We most keenly felt his absence in the winter of 1951. Heavy rains had caused flooding and landslides. They had felled trees and washed-out roads. Nina and I drove up to see the extent of the damage. As we approached the turnoff, we realized it would be impossible to take the car down that seven-tenths of a mile into camp. Rain, now more like icy sleet, was still falling, and water gushed over mud-filled ruts. With Nina's collection of hand tools in the trunk of her car, we sloshed and slid every few feet to the lodge. After a few cups of hot coffee, we donned our jeans, boots, oil slickers, and hoods. Each of us armed with a shovel, we started pushing back dirt, mud, twigs, and gravel. As I ran my fingers down the ditch, clearing away the slime, wet clay seeped under my fingernails and stuck to my hands. Squatting, we hacked away for what seemed hours.

"Next thing we raise money for," I said, feeling pitifully inadequate for this miserable job, "is paving this road."

In town, we were astonished to discover how much that ambition would cost: five thousand dollars. But as usual, the Enchanted Hills angels were still working their magic. A local foundation agreed to pay half the bill if we could find someone to match it. One of our board members came forward with the required $2,500 and within a year the camp had its paved road.

Every season brought some crisis. During our first year a fire broke out at a resort three miles away. Clumps of smoke drifted threateningly close, so Nina sent the word out to pile the campers into the station wagon and counselors' cars and drive down to Angie's, a coffee shop five miles down the road. There we found Brother Gregory from the nearby Christian Brothers Winery. When he heard our plight, he invited all of us—sixteen staff and forty children—to spend the night there.

Besides a sumptuous meal, the brothers gave us a tour of the winery, including generous samples. Observing several children after the fourth or fifth, the counselors hustled off to bed a collection of droopy, docile youngsters.

As it turned out, members of the fire department, aided by local volunteers, helped contain the fire. Our next project was the installation of fire-safety equipment around every building and in every area of the camp.

The children were a cross-section of race, creed, and culture and came, for the most part, from poor and sad backgrounds. Some had been left on doorsteps at birth, others had grown up in institutions, and many had known only foster homes.

Such a child was ten-year-old Lettie Brig. Camp was obviously her first group living experience, and she hated everybody and everything about it. She resented the idea of coming to meals at regular times and having to wait her turn for Nina's hand-inspection before entering the mess hall. She ate with her fingers and saw no reason to change her socks every day or use a toothbrush each morning. When she could not have her way, she spewed out obscenities. The staff tried to find ways of helping Lettie become a better person—not an easy undertaking in two weeks.

One day they almost sent her home. In a running relay game she stood behind a colored boy.

"Goddamn, I'm not standing back of no nigger," she screamed.

Her living-unit counselor talked long and seriously with her, warning that she would have to leave unless she apologized to Jimmy. Despite her complaints, Lettie had no desire to cut short her vacation. It was better than home. She did apologize, and the staff decided to let her stay.

In the session's final reports, her living-unit counselor wrote, "Lettie learned to flush a toilet, use deodorant, and brush her teeth and hair. Of knives and forks she still says, 'Them's only for city folk.' Her favorite activities were knocking down the tin cans we used for bowling pins and toasting marshmallows."

With the help of the Twenty-Thirty Club, Casey, Herb's replacement, installed plastic guidelines at fifteen-foot intervals over waist-high redwood posts. These helped campers walk, and more often run, from place to place. When they smelled mint, they knew that the ranch house was near. The sound of the nearby stream told them they were approaching the chapel.

Each cabin selected a representative to serve on the camp council. It met twice weekly with the program director to plan activities or revise schedules. It might recommend fewer hikes, a recorded talent show, or a moonlight swim. At the meetings they discovered the hard realities of program planning, the difficulty of providing fare acceptable to all. They learned to set aside their own preferences for the will of the majority, to organize and plan ahead. They improved their ability to express themselves and gained in poise, in self-confidence, and in a new awareness of their own potentials. Some developed qualities of leadership. Listening in on these sessions from time to time, I could hear them growing.

Some campers had never been out of the city before. For them camp was a revelation. On hikes they explored the bottoms of stream beds, rock formations, and other geologic phenomena. They developed a kind of foot intelligence, learning to distinguish between types of terrain, angle of earth incline, how to step on and over rocks, pebbles, plowed ground, sand. They touched the fronds of a fern, the strata of rocks, and branches of trees. They listened for the sound of birds, brooks, insects, animals, and the wind. From these and the fragrance of pine, bay, honeysuckle, and mint, they formed a composite picture of the trail, rich and varied. They hiked in pairs or threes, teaming up with a partially sighted friend or one of the leaders.

Counselors showed them the tracks of deer, skunk, and raccoon. On the way to chapel the campers stopped to touch lichens, fungi, spider webs, birds' nests, and pine cones. Some brought back specimens for the "what-is-it" shelf in the camp museum, or to keep for surprises on treasure-hunt nights.

"Come and see a new visitor," a counselor said one day to a group gathered in Redwood Circle.

"What is it, what is it?" they wanted to know, some of the boys jumping up, the girls hanging back, since this leader was always gathering up odd specimens for their amusement and sometimes consternation. Five or six lads crowded round her, reaching out to touch a long, scaly body with, of all things, a bulge halfway down its length.

"Oh boy, a nice snake," they squealed delightedly. "But what's that big fat part?"

"Guess he's just had a big dinner," suggested the counselor. "Let's put him in a bucket and cover him up for the night."

Next morning an even larger group of campers gathered round to see the creature. There, next to the mother, they found six baby snakes. It took considerable persuasion to let the new family return to its home.

For many children, camp afforded the first opportunity to touch rabbits, chickens, horses, cows, sheep, and pigs. On occasion Casey would charm the children by inviting them to help him gather eggs, feed the ducks, or try for fish in one of the camp creeks.

One counselor used a dressmaker's wheel and Braille slate to make a raised map of the stars visible in the night during the camp season. A specially written text by Dr. Alma Wittlin, with illustrative paper cutouts labeled in Braille, described the leaves of trees indigenous to Enchanted Hills. Three children discovered that a family of robins had made a nest in the corner of their cabin. By the end of two weeks, they saw the fledglings grow fat on their feeding and loving care.

The campers planted a lemon tree and year after year watched the blossoms and fruit grow. They took turns using the Rototiller in the vegetable garden and in gathering carrots, onions, tomatoes, or squash or, as they ripened, apples, walnuts, and plums in the orchard. Sometimes the campers brought back wild flowers to decorate dining room tables.

When Rex Mason, president of the Potters of America, was our crafts counselor, all manner of marvelous surprises came out of the hobby shop. The kilns and pottery wheels were busy night and day. The boys and girls made clay animals, ashtrays, and pots. From the native materials—oak, redwood, madrone—they fashioned candlestick holders and lamp bases. They made copper bracelets, cloth utility bags, felt flowers, leather wallets, wooden trays, and clogs.

When they had learned to hammer, drill, saw, and sand, they made miniature sailboats to float in the wading pool. In one session, the teenagers produced a huge raft. They had intended to launch it, but it proved unseaworthy and was christened the *Ivy Leak*.

The pool area was the first to be improved. We replaced the old wooden deck with concrete, planted lawn where there had been brambles and blackberry weeds, installed modern showers and toilets, and bordered the oaks and maples that framed the pool with pink and purple oleanders. Each year the Davis auxiliary put fresh paint on the aquamarine pool floor and sides.

"Let's get on the tubes." "I'm gonna practice with the kickboard." "Lemme go under your legs." "I'll race you to the end of the pool." Squeals, shouts, bubble-blowing, splashes, a hurdle, a back dive, a jackknife dive—these were the sounds of unmitigated joy and freedom I heard at the pool. Those who were able to meet the standard qualifications received Red Cross Beginners', Intermediate, or Life-Saving cards.

Every camper learned to row. The more ambitious competed in boat races, occasions of uproarious rivalry. Microphone in hand, Nina refereed. She had carved notches on the underside of the handles to keep the oars straight. A bell at the far end of the lake informed the contestants of the accuracy and speed with which they were approaching the goal and whether or not they were on course.

Horseback-riding really sent campers' temperatures soaring. Many campers had never seen a horse; now they could touch his mane, ears, withers, and hooves. No one was allowed to ride until he had groomed his horse. We prevailed upon Nina to take time out from the office for the "Bronco Billies." Under her supervision, beginning riders first learned to control their horses in the ring. From there they graduated to the baseball diamond and finally the trails, learning to trot, canter, and gallop in good form. Somehow they frequently connived to ride past the kitchen for a secret handout.

The campers played baseball in a special way. The pitcher rolled the ball to the batter. When he heard it coming toward him along the dirt, he knelt and hit it. Then, to the sound of handclapping and of the basemen calling, "Come on, Dick, come on, Dick," the runners circled the bases. The games were as wild, and the teams as competitive, as any in the World Series.

And there were other equally exciting games. In kickball, distance-kicking was the basis of point-scoring. Some of the campers liked to bowl, using logs to form an alley, and cans for pins. Relays, squat tag, and musical chairs were standard field day fun. On rainy days, they played Braille cards, scrabble, bingo, and shuffleboard. In checkers, square and round shapes differentiated black from white.

But the favorite teenage activity was social dancing. On Wednesday and Saturday nights preparations for the dances in the big barn were feverish. All day the girls ironed dresses, shampooed and curled their hair. The boys lined up their partners.

Every year Enchanted Hillers clamored for the upside-down costume party. Campers and staff wore socks on their ears, shoes around their necks, pants inside out. I dressed Toddy, my dog, in my shorts and draped her harness around my neck. Nina was the official commentator, but some campers preferred to see for themselves.

Enchanted Hills was a singing camp. We sang in the dining room after breakfast, on the trails during hikes, around the campfire, in the cabins and in chapel. When the campers first arrived they sang as individuals—each one at his own tempo, pitch, and volume—but by the third day their voices blended and they were singing as a group. They acquired a tremendous repertoire of folk tunes, gesture songs, and spirituals. They sang in unison, in harmony, in rounds; some in French, Spanish, and Italian.

On Sunday mornings, staff and campers in their starched blouses and fresh shorts gathered in front of the mess hall and reverently walked together in pairs through the woods and across the little bridge to their green cathedral. Campers sat on the tiered logs, the choir remaining up front to lead in the United Nations Song of Peace, "Jacob's Ladder," "Dona Nobis Pacem," and the camp theme song, "No Man Is an Island."

Sometimes a guitar, flute, recorder, autoharp, or violin, depending on what talent was present in the session, added to the music of the gushing creek, the birds, the wind, and the trees. There was no sermon. Campers chose their favorite texts from "Altars Under the Sky," "Services in the Open," the Old or New Testaments, or other prose and poetry. One Sunday morning one camper read from the camp nature book:

> Every new friend brings new riches to our life—his personal interests and knowledge, his concerns and hopes, his readiness to share our own problems and joys. Life's stream flows deeper and stronger the more we know of others and of our mutual dependence upon each other. This wonderful fellowship links not only all men and women, boys and girls, but it knits us human beings together with all other forms of the universe—with the rocks under our

feet and the stars above our heads, with all the four-legged and winged creatures in fur and feather, with the life that pulses in the seas, and with the silent green world around us, the world of plants.

After Tim had finished reading, he surprised the assembled group: "And now I would like to say that to me Enchanted Hills is a place where the sun and moon are happy to shine. This is a place where God can look down and see his children working and playing together. This is a place where the trees sing, a place of peace and joy."

At the close of each camp season, Nina and I received eloquent letters from parents, counselors, and campers but the most poignant came in Braille from Dick Wells after his first experience at Enchanted Hills:

> At camp I learned to sit up straighter at meals, and that in this life one must give as well as take. When I learned how to row and pitch horseshoes, I felt proud. All these things have helped me to become happy since my life is now more filled. All in all, camp has meant a lot of fun to me—it has taught me many things, but most of all it has made me feel more wanted by people.

Of all my years at camp, the 1956 teenage session will always be most vivid in my memory. The fine staff; the buoyant camp spirit; the competent kitchen crew; the abundant equipment, supplies, and food; the glorious weather—every element necessary to an ideal camp was present.

In a flash one day I thought, "This session must somehow be preserved. Now that we have enough in the treasury, why not arrange for a really good film?" We engaged Moulin Studios in San Francisco to take movies of the camp in action. Mrs. Robert Gordon Sproul, wife of the former president of the University of California and member of our board of directors, persuaded Irene Dunne to narrate the movie.

During the filming we had difficulty keeping some of the curious teenagers from tampering with the equipment. But the boys and girls were endlessly patient about posing, repeating scenes and songs until the timing was perfect. Ralph, demonstrating his lifesaving test, dove into the pool five times fully dressed. The campfire had to be laid several times before the photographer was satisfied with the lighting.

Thus Enchanted Hills opened a whole new dimension of growth for blind children and adults. For some, it meant added zest in living, for others new fields of study. Camp inspired many to take up their present vocations: they work successfully as folk-singers, recreation-leaders, craftsmen.

I suppose this was the happiest period of my career. If only Alma Guy and Ida May could have been there to see it! The mechanics of the organization were running smooth as silk. Money was pouring in—the five-dollar and ten-dollar donations had become twenty-five and fifty, a hundred, a thousand. We were getting more and more legacies, and in big chunks.

I loved my work not only for its success and recognition, for the growth it meant to children, and for the joy to adults, but also for its exhilaration, the pace and creativity it demanded, the variety of my responsibilities, the people such a project attracted, and above all, the realization of purpose in living.

No longer did I wonder why I was in this world. The

future beckoned for still greater achievement. Ahead lay brilliant prospects. The next step would be a year-round rehabilitation center in town such as the world had never seen. All the right portents were there.

[19]

An Unfinished Opera

AFTER RUDY'S year in Switzerland, one of the happiest of his life, he had returned to New York only to find every avenue of work closed to him. As I had feared, Columbia Community Concerts had blacklisted him for breach of contract. He could not return to his teaching job, since the Manhattan School of Music had hired its faculty for the year.

His spirits were at an all-time low until, early in 1950, he accepted a post on the faculty of Louisiana State University. He wrote glowingly of the beauty of the campus, its exotic flowers and trees, but complained that coaching opera students and playing recitals left him little time for what he loved most: composing. An ironic fate was to bring him the opportunity he craved.

Late the following spring I received a letter saying that he planned to vacation in California. "I'm going to spend a few days at the Ananda Ashrama, not far from Los Angeles. But first I want to see you. It's been too long. So unless something unexpected occurs I'll be there about the last of July or the early part of August."

Rudy coming to Enchanted Hills! Somehow I had never thought this would happen. The thought of him as a romantic part of my life had long since been buried. However, with this news, old memories stirred, and a little thrill of anticipation ran through all the early summer days until he arrived the morning of August 1.

Hearing his voice, I hurried out to the gate.

"Rose," he cried, "you're brown as a berry."

"You're actually here," I said, throwing my arms around him. "I can't believe it."

He immediately got off to a bad start with Nina by asking, "Can someone take these bags to my room? My hands, you know—can't take a chance of hurting them." Disgusted that anyone should be so spoiled, virtuoso or not, Nina picked up the bags herself and whisked them off in a huff.

From time to time, I had sent him clippings about the camp; now that he could see the beauty of the setting, the joy of the children, he was deeply moved. On the way to his tent he said, "It's beautiful beyond anything I imagined."

That evening he played a concert on the old upright piano in the Lodge. Every person in the camp had gathered for the unusual treat. Nina was so captivated by his playing that she forgave him his self-indulgence.

Rarely had I taken time for personal pleasure. It had been so long since I had seen Rudy that I spent every available moment with him. All else became secondary. I could hardly wait for my free time to see him. Our being together made me realize how starved I had been for someone to talk to about things that interested me personally.

When I was not on duty, he gave me long tough lessons, reviewing old repertoire and teaching me his own "Cascades" and "Christ's Weary Journey." He played for me the two completed movements of his *Alpine* Concerto, begun in Switzerland, the strongest and most dramatic, I thought, of all his compositions.

Sometimes on walks along the lilac trail back of Casey's old house, or in deep woods, we would find a peaceful spot where he would read to me passages from books he had brought along.

Even in the maelstrom of New York he had always surrounded himself with a cloak of serenity. It was still there and I felt my body and mind, parts I hadn't realized were clenched and tense, gradually relaxing.

On his second night at camp, as we lingered by the fire in the lodge for a round of songs, he leaned close to me and whispered, "Couldn't we slip off by ourselves? There's a gorgeous full moon."

So we found our favorite spot, a tree-sheltered dell bordering the chapel. Dew accentuated the perfume of juniper, fir, and redwood. The stillness was broken only by the sound of the nearby brook and the occasional chirp of a cricket. The moon was so bright that, astonished almost beyond belief, I could see its light spilling through the branches over our heads.

"Let's stay here a while, shall we?" Rudy said.

I took off my red cardigan to sit on, and Rudy dropped down beside me.

"I wish I could take this peace back to the university. There are so many students around and so little time for privacy or meditation. I continue to be plagued with attacks of depression."

"Well, if you mean moods or spells, everyone has those."

"No, it's not like that. It's a feeling of utter depletion and hopelessness."

"Do they come when you aren't producing, when ideas and themes don't come as readily as you want them to?"

"Yes, partly that."

"Well, that's true of all creative people, isn't it?"

"I don't know, but let's not talk about it. I just want you to know that coming here, seeing you in this setting, being alone with you, has shaken me out of one."

He took me in his arms.

"Rudy!" I breathed, melting, smothering my surprise. Feelings of admiration and affection, long sublimated, suddenly ignited. Whether it was our shared perceptions of the beauty and mystery around us, or some inner need, long dormant in both of us, there in the forest we became more than teacher and pupil. His voice, usually firm and flat, took on a hushed, tender quality.

"I should have come long ago—I've wanted to." He pressed hard against me until we were both stretched full length on the ground.

Rudy, the restrained, remote, mystical Rudy was loving me with all the intensity of the *Appassionata* Sonata —kissing my neck, my breasts, my eyes, my lips, filling me with an almost unbearable excitement. His touch, his quickening breath, his tight closeness drew me into his being, him into mine.

"I—love you—my God!"

Was that my voice? Strange—but yes, it was me, a me emerging from long ago, a me that had long since wrapped up passion as an irrelevant, unviable part of my life, expressible only in music and in my work. And now, with Rudy, I was surrendering to a more elemental energy, an accelerating force sweeping us on, out of self, out of time and space until we were at peace—simultaneously at peace. Then silence—both of us quite still. Then again, quietly now, Rudy's mouth was on mine.

"Dearest," he whispered, "I always knew from your playing how it would be."

Then, floating ... gliding ... we drifted off on feathers of sleep.

He asked me next day if I would come down to the city for his last night before going south. Up to this time I had never been away overnight while camp was in session. Now, nothing could deter me from this happiness.

In perfect tune with our mood, the movie *Cyrano de Bergerac* was playing in town. We went to the six o'clock show, then had dinner in the Tonga Room of the Fairmont Hotel. We shared a South Seas cocktail and a Cantonese dinner and danced to the Hawaiian band. In the middle of a languorous waltz, Rudy murmured, "I'd love to take you back to Spiez with me some day."

"Promise you'll write whenever you're depressed."

"I won't wait till then."

At my apartment, both of us automatically drifted to the piano, Rudy to the keyboard.

"You're going to sit there and play all my favorites," I commanded.

"All right. Fire away."

I feasted on the Brahms F Minor Sonata, the Mozart A Major Sonata, and Rosenthal's "Papillons." He was playing at concert pitch!

"I should have turned my recorder on," I said.

"I'll make some tapes for you when I get back to Baton Rouge."

I thought he had earned an intermission. "Rudy," I asked, "what is this Vedanta retreat you're going to in La Crescenta?"

"It's a peaceful place—perfect for a rest, in the hills north of Los Angeles—a lovely setting in the midst of trees, shrubs, and flowers. My cousins, Jo and Otto, who live in Pacific Palisades, took me there once and I've always wanted to go back. They have daily services and periods of meditation."

"Just what are their beliefs?" I asked.

"Well, for one thing, they regard the world as illusion, Maya. They believe the Hindu scriptures contain the foundation of all creeds, that man is essentially pure and that if he can control his desire for material things, he has within himself the power to be master of his destiny and ultimately to reach divine perfection."

"Do you agree with that?"

"Tagore expresses my sentiments in one of his poems when he said, 'Deliverance is not for me in renunciation.'" He got up and came over to sit beside me on the sofa. "And you—" he asked, punctuating his words with kisses, "what do you think about desire?"

"I—I think it's—basic to man's quest for perfection and self-perpetuation. I'm thinking of desire in the broadest sense, not restricted to amorous fulfillment."

And so we talked and loved throughout the night, wondering if our being together were real.

After breakfast the next morning I showed Rudy some of my favorite places in Golden Gate Park: the eucalyptus groves, the Shakespeare Garden, a meadow by the lake. It was a golden, buoyant day. We walked for hours.

An Unfinished Opera

After a noon snack at El Portal, we tramped across town to the palace of the Legion of Honor, arriving in time to hear part of a lecture on impressionist painting. We had to leave before it was over so that Rudy could catch his plane.

We took a bus home, and while he bathed and dressed I went to the piano to try over what he had taught me of "Cascades."

Finally, he was ready. I walked with him to the door. We stood, quiet and close, in a long embrace.

"My own true love," he whispered, and was gone.

His words filled me with a quiet elation, an emotion wholly new to me, the nearest to a religious feeling I had ever experienced. For several seconds I stood motionless, hearing again the power and beauty of his music—passion directed and controlled by a lucid mind, the mark of a true artist.

Then slowly the old world, the world I had shed for a few days, crept back into my consciousness. This was no world for a creative spirit. All its mores and values were in conflict with his nature and temperament. What he had said after his breakup with his pianist wife, Marlowe Lane, flashed back: "If anyone catches me planning to get married again, I hope they shoot me."

I was thankful that I felt no need to possess him. It was enough to know that for now, near or far, we would inhabit each other's minds and senses. I was still obsessed with the memory of our days together. I couldn't get him out of my mind. I wrote him:

> Words cannot describe the deep, sweet pleasure of having you with me these past few days. Thank you for letting me drink at the fountain of your spirit

and mind. Your departure would leave an emptiness were it not for all you left me to absorb. Besides, I have only to refer to my heart to find you.

And after five tremulous days, Rudy replied:

Now, almost a week later, I am still under the spell of our last two days together. Life has rarely if ever brought sweeter moments. My thoughts all day are little else than dreams of you. You have created a new retreat in my mind.

A few days later, on his way to Baton Rouge, he stopped at the Grand Canyon and wrote me from the Shrine of the Ages about his visit to the Ashrama.

He and Sister Daya, head of the retreat, had had long discussions about religion, art, and music. He happened to mention a Walter Hampden performance of *The Light of Asia,* a play based on the life of Buddha, produced in New York and Hollywood in 1929, and had been astonished to learn that Sister Daya, formerly Georgiana Walton Jones, was the author of the play. Learning that Rudy admired it greatly, and hearing him play some of his compositions, Sister Daya invited him to stay at the Ashrama for an indefinite period. Impractical Rudy had agreed to make the play into an opera merely for room and board. Moreover he had also agreed to turn over to the Ashrama all his worldly possessions. It would mean resigning from the university after the next semester. He wrote:

It's like being commissioned, only better. I won't have the pressure of having to finish on a certain date. It's the realization of my longest most cher-

An Unfinished Opera

ished dream—and to think it will mean being close to you!

At the end of May the following year he resigned from Louisiana State University and moved to the Ananda Ashrama. Early in July he wrote:

> If someone handed me a quarter of a million dollars and told me to build a place, I couldn't have excelled this. It's ideal for creative work. I can't wait to show it to you. I can't believe that God has made it possible for me to live in this beautiful place. But why should I be surprised when even before that He gave me your love? I pray daily to be worthy of that. When can you come?

I flew down for a weekend in mid-August. Rudy was at the airport.

"Marvelous to have you here," he said. "I've been planning the things we'll do while you're here." He took my bag, not too heavy for his hands this time, as we walked toward the limousine.

"I was so excited about your coming, I couldn't sleep last night."

"Will you have time to work at the piano?" I asked.

"I definitely planned to. First, we'll review the things you'd like to play for me, then I hope you'll ask me to play some of the recordings of the L.S.U. concert, and of course, there are a million things to read and more than that to talk about. In fact, I made a two-page list last night. I want to hear all about the camp, and be sure to remind me to report on *The Song of Norway* and the Ruth St. Denis recital."

He was thoughtful at every turn, showing me around my room and the grounds, introducing me to the sisters and some of the guests. We attended one of the services, and when it was time for sacred meditation, I fell into a sweet fantasy about Rudy.

The place felt like the home of the dead. People moved like shadows. Their handshakes were lifeless. They talked in whispers, and the conversation consisted of an occasional comment about the weather. I concluded it must be the setting, the gardens, and the trees which were hypnotizing Rudy.

On the way back to the residence building after lunch, I admitted, "The food reminds me of the Cowler meals on the road. I'm still hungry."

"I have some chocolate in my room."

"But Rudy, how can you work with such meager meals?"

"Most of us eat too much. Your stomach shrinks with less intake and you work better."

"Rudy," I ventured, "have you done any work on the opera?"

"No, I want to thoroughly saturate myself with the play. It has everything in it of spectacular and profound drama, from the secular seductive dancing of Oriental harem girls to the sacred moment of Buddha's illumination in a Himalayan forest. Colossal! And with your constant inspiration I know I'll be able to do it."

But he never wrote the opera. A perfectionist, he had embarked on exhaustive researches of Buddha's life and influence, the origins and evolution of opera and Indian music. Only an occasional song, a hymn for the Ashrama, came from his pen.

Whether it was the atmosphere of the retreat, his dwindling finances, a paralyzing fear, or a bog of self-doubt, he fell into an acute depression. His next letter threw me into a panic.

> Precious: I reached a low point last night—I hope the lowest of this life. It's as though I had fallen down a ten-thousand-foot precipice in a matter of seconds, and now I'm struggling up a winding and pathless wilderness that seems to have more downward than upward grades. I went through the tortures of the damned in the preparation of three programs, practicing as largo as possible. And thank God I got through the recital for three different audiences without a single memory slip.
>
> Those terrible depressed feelings have hit me again and I am beginning to feel that I am waging a losing battle. Most of the time I feel desperate about being able to hold out. Of late, I've been plagued by thoughts of suicide—there have been many minutes in recent months I have not been **able** to get the thought out of my mind. I don't feel **safe**. I know this will worry you and I ask for your forgiveness. My only justification is that, in knowing it, you may be able to prevent it. The only other person I have shared these feelings with is my sister, Olive. I would long since have fallen under had it not been for her help, my music and your love and belief in me. If I should suddenly phone you, could you or would you come? I don't seem to be able to make the spiritual connection that I've had most of my life. I feel ashamed to burden you with this. I'll try to believe that my telling you will be for the best.
>
> *Love eternal, Rudy*

I rushed to talk the situation over with Nina, and we agreed to drive to Los Angeles immediately. We found Rudy emaciated, his spirit gone. We took him to a quiet place for dinner, but he hardly tasted his food.

I tried to revive his will to participate in life and to use his gifts, suggesting that he try for teaching posts at U.C.L.A. and U.S.C. and for appearances in radio or television. But he listened apathetically, and I knew he couldn't summon enough will to take any initiative.

As we drove back to the Ashrama, Nina asked, "How long is it, Rudy, since you had a complete medical? This depression may be due to some physical drain. You know we don't separate mind from body any more."

"Oh," he said, "I've been that route. My cousin Jo is a nurse, you know, and she made me go through all that, months ago. I draw the line at psychiatrists. Those fellows just pull you apart and don't know how to put the pieces back together again. I don't think it's connected to any situation—it just seems to be part of my nature, born in my blood, I suppose."

"You've written to your sister, Olive?" I asked.

"Yes, she wants to come out right away."

"Rudy, that would be wonderful," I said. "But we want to take you back to camp—just until you get the taste of this place out of your system. Would you consider it?"

"Oh," he said vaguely, "the camp is so peaceful, so beautiful. But you don't want a dying horse around."

"Rudy, that's nonsense," Nina said. "You come back with us and you won't feel that way long."

I suggested that he explain to Sister Daya that the financial arrangement had proven inadequate, or better still, that he move away. I was sure his family would help him get back on his feet. But his response was limp and indifferent.

A great knot of foreboding swelled in my throat. It was agony to hold back the tears. The way he was living, without pay, withdrawn from life, was bound to wither his self-confidence. It was as though the reality of an unseen world slowly overshadowed the world without.

Before beginning his work on the opera, he felt that he must prepare himself by performing various offices, meditate upon the emptiness and nonexistence of all things until he lost all consciousness of self and was able to identify himself with Divinity. He attended two daily one-hour sessions of meditation. This excessive introspection apparently walled him in from reality, and was in direct conflict with his temperament as an artist and his full, free life in New York. Instead of concerts, the theater, gallery visits, and the stimulation of other creative people, he was limited to the cloistered environment of the Ashrama. Moreover, the sisters, who had promised not to pressure him, became impatient with his several starts and slow progress with the opera.

Rudy had had a productive life of teaching, composing, performing. He had taught at Juilliard as well as the Manhattan School of Music, had made four coast-to-coast tours of the United States, and had given concerts in Europe, Australia, New Zealand, Canada, India, Burma, and Ceylon. He had appeared with the National, Philadelphia, New York, and N.B.C. Symphony orchestras, receiving rave press notices everywhere. He had published some seventy pieces for piano, violin, and voice. And now, at this Vedantist retreat, the place where he had expected to see the fulfillment of his most cherished dream, the well of energy refused to flow. The muse refused to speak.

Nina and I were convinced that a month at the camp would restore him and that he must permanently move away from the Ashrama. His cousins, Jo and Otto, welcomed him to live with them if he so desired after his return from camp.

We were relieved, finally, to find Rudy amenable to the plan. On the drive back from La Crescenta, we promised him that there would be no demands on him socially, that he could practice, write, read, participate in activities, swim, ride, row, hike—be entirely free. At the end of one month, he had improved enough to play a superb benefit recital for Recreation at the California Club in San Francisco. We had a hard time persuading him to take even a third of the proceeds.

Upon his return to southern California he lived for a while with his cousins, then took an apartment in Santa Monica. He had one parting blow at the hands of the sisters—they refused to let him have his Steinway grand piano. Rudy never complained about it, apparently believing that this, his most precious possession, was an expected sacrifice when he went to live there.

In the ensuing years I saw him only sporadically. He would spend weekends with me now and then in the city. He was calm and vital again. He had regained enough health and stability to be playing in public at his old level of excellence, sometimes as soloist, sometimes with a Hollywood ensemble.

Early one morning in the fall of 1965 he dropped into my apartment, full of vigor. He insisted on scrambling some eggs with, of all things, slices of cantaloupe he

An Unfinished Opera

found in the refrigerator. I thought it tasted silly, but Rudy downed it with relish.

"Darling," he said, "I have wonderful news! I've finished my *Alpine* Concerto. Why don't you premiere it with the Los Angeles Symphony?"

"Marvelous," I said, "but not for me. I don't get to the piano often enough these days for that. It needs a virtuoso. Why don't you do it?"

That idea he left hanging, but went on to an equally exciting surprise. "I'm making plans," he said, "for you to climb Mount Whitney with me." Would we, I wondered, be able to recapture the happiness we had known before?

We were never to find out.

Only two weeks later, Otto wrote that at a friend's house where Rudy had been invited for dinner, he complained of a headache. The friend suggested that he lie down, and continued preparing the meal. When, a few minutes later, she looked in on him, he had slipped to the floor. He had no pulse. It was Rudy's finale: a cerebral vascular accident.

His had been a cruel and ironic life. He was an authentic genius who had reached the height of his profession. Then, by some caprice of fate, he had been cheated out of its fruits. His death left me with a haunting sense of loss. I was grateful that he had lived to finish his Concerto, performed by the Harrisburg Symphony Orchestra four years after his death. The Juilliard School houses his bust. The Library of Congress has added his works to the catalogue of American composers.

During Rudy's lifetime it was his custom to jot down his philosophical thoughts and beliefs. He left behind two volumes called *Spiritual Revelations*.

Found on his desk at the time of his death, on a small sheet of music paper (no doubt meant for the collection) were these words:

"My spirit has found its eternal home in harmony with the Great Silence." They have been chiseled on his headstone in Bellefontaine Cemetery, in St. Louis, where he was born.

[20]

A Fatal Decision

Now that the camp was established and running smoothly my thoughts went back to the old dream of a San Francisco Lighthouse such as I had known as a child in New York. Blindcraft was still operating as a nineteenth-century broom shop. The center was still serving up busywork. I began urging the board of directors of Recreation for the Blind to acquire its own in-town headquarters, suitable for a comprehensive program of rehabilitation, social service, and recreation. Finding the board favorable to the idea, I obtained permission from my alma mater to use the name "San Francisco Lighthouse."

Mrs. June Ososke, wife of a city official, arranged for a showing of "A Day at Enchanted Hills" for her American Legion Auxiliary. While the film was still running, she leaned over and whispered, "How would you like me to start an auxiliary for your organization?"

"June, do you really mean it? We have a project crying out for just such help. At the last meeting the board approved a plan to find a site for permanent headquarters."

In the ensuing months June organized a group of thirty women whose annual contributions to Recreation provided the down payment on 45,000 square feet of space in central San Francisco, where Recreation put up a sign: "Future Home of the San Francisco Lighthouse for the Blind."

For some time businessmen in the community, as well as members of the board, had been urging Recreation to consolidate with Blindcraft and the Buchanan Street Center.

"Right now," they maintained, "there are three fund-raising drives for the blind. Why not consolidate and streamline this effort? You'd have more money to work with and be able to do a bigger job."

It sounded reasonable to me. By pooling our resources, services would be centralized, therefore more effective. It would eliminate the need for people to shop from one agency to another for help. Besides, after ten years of year-round fund-raising, I would be able to devote more time to programs.

But when I talked it over with Nina, I found her violently opposed to the idea.

"Think of the work it would save us in promotion every year," I said. "There'd be just one concerted drive instead of several competing appeals to the public. We could put all that time and energy into a worthwhile year-round program in town."

"Rose, I think you are making a big mistake. We have a marvelous project, successful in every way. The reason it's been a success is that our board gives us complete freedom to run the organization. Merge, and you'll only inherit all the troubles of Blindcraft and the center. And they'll buck you all the way."

"But this town has never had a decent program for the blind, and even with our own building I don't think we could bring it off alone—financially, I mean."

"I'm not interested in any rehabilitation program. We do the real job at camp. I don't think we should take on any more."

"My idea would be to hire other people to supervise each department."

"What makes you think we'd have any say about hiring?"

"You mean you don't trust our board to protect our position in the organization?"

"That's right. I certainly don't."

"Oh Nina, they couldn't let us down. People all over the state know what we've put into this work."

This was our first major disagreement. In some ways it was understandable. Whereas Nina had stumbled into social welfare through our friendship, I had elected it as the answer to my need for a purpose in life. Nina treasured our freedom and security in the organization and was certain we would come up against the same bureaucratic attitudes and internecine jealousies we had encountered in the building of our project. To me consolidation was a challenge to yet greater achievement. She had no desire to get any bigger.

Yet if, as the businessmen claimed, it was in the best interests of the blind to consolidate, weren't we obliged to do so? With our Lighthouse sign up on the new property, weren't we committed to the development of a multiservice agency? William Mosell, architect on the board, had drawn plans for the building.

Always in the past, Nina and I had submitted recommendations with one mind, and the board had followed our wishes. Now, seeing our difference of opinion, the board took matters into its own hands. It voted to consolidate Enchanted Hills with the Center for the Blind and Blindcraft.

To both of us, the signing of the papers was painful—it marked the end of an era in our lives, a time of phenomenal success and deep gratification. The self-contained, indestructible Nina wept.

Recreation turned over to the newly formed agency contributor mailing lists, nine auxiliaries, the $50,000 building site in central San Francisco, cash from legacies amounting to upwards of $200,000, and the camp itself, appraised at $250,000.

Each of the former agencies—Enchanted Hills, Blindcraft, and the center—became departments in the new organization, the San Francisco Lighthouse for the Blind, incorporated in February 1958.

Instead of naming an executive, the board designated three of its members as the administrative committee to run the new agency. Ed Rohl, former contractor, became supervisor of Blindcraft; Mr. Pence continued as director of the Center; Nina remained camp director. Only my responsibilities were completely changed. The committee assigned me to the direction of program and public relations. My office was to be at Blindcraft, my old stand! Furthermore, the Committee put my new job in crushing terms: "You are to have nothing to do with the camp."

What an ominous beginning in the new order! A

stinging blow right off. I felt robbed, cheated—an exile from the project to which I had given ten years of my life. Were they saying that I was no longer needed at the camp—the camp I had regarded as my purpose in living? It had been the embodiment of my ideals, almost an extension of my being—the trees, the flowers, the water, the air, the wildlife, the children's laughter—the transformations I had seen in their lives, the music, the peace of campfire and chapel. Never to know these again was a kind of death I was not certain I could endure. But bitter pill as it was, I knew I had to swallow it.

I had to force myself to use reason. After all, I was reacting in a personal way. When you came right down to it, what more was there to be done for the camp? All the procedures—administration, program, housing, camper recruitment and registration, staffing, transportation for children and adults, fund-raising, press relations, professional contacts—all had been established. Perhaps I had done as much as I could for the camp and it was time to move on to the bigger dream.

Separation from the camp brought home to me the realization that I was no longer an executive. I was now an employee, expected to take orders. Well, I told myself, you asked for it. You wanted a Lighthouse. You were the one who trusted these people. Now you must bear the brunt. Here is the chance to make the Lighthouse you envisioned a reality. With a resolute mind, I tried to turn off my feelings and bolster the will to succeed in the new arena.

The administrative committee's job proved more complicated than its members had bargained for. None of them knew anything about blindness; few visited the facilities or were familiar with the day-to-day problems.

The staff was obliged to await monthly board meetings for approval of policy, procedure, or petty cash expenditures. No one had authority to act. There was no sense of unity. The agency was like a ship without a rudder. There was no communication between staff members and the board, and very little between the department heads. Clients were registering complaints with kitchen personnel and board members, a situation which undermined the position of the staff, delayed action, and caused anxiety and apprehension among the clients and conflict and confusion within and between departments.

In approaching my first assignment in the new régime, I decided that both program and public relations needed a complete overhaul, or more accurately, a fresh start. But before any changes could be made, the board must learn exactly what was going on in the various departments. They must agree on some philosophy, some objectives by which to design program and measure performance. They must provide for public accountability.

While Enchanted Hills could present detailed records dating back to 1947, neither of the other departments had kept any account of their operations. Therefore, I sent questionnaires to Pence at the center, and Rohl at Blindcraft, asking for a description of the attendance and activities in their respective departments. The completed questionnaire from Pence revealed that the center still accommodated some fifty blind people, many of them the same elderly men and women I had collected for the Lions sixteen years earlier. Their activities continued to be Braille, monthly dances, and free lunches. The center was open only from ten to three weekdays, never on weekends.

Rohl's filled-in questionnaire showed that Blindcraft

employed sixteen broom-makers, ten of whom had been there twenty years, six for thirty. Conditions for the workers were virtually the same as I had observed them twenty years earlier: Some were paid by piecework, others earned fifty cents an hour, and there were frequent layoffs. Brooms were still the major item of production and sporadic contracts with private wholesalers the only marketing outlets. Floors squeaked; plumbing dated back to 1925; a huge auditorium and practically the whole third floor were scarcely used.

In addition to recommending repair of physical facilities, my report stated:

> Both the center and Blindcraft are currently operating as instruments of segregation and dependency. The agency is nowhere in contact with the public—that is to say, there exists no dialogue or working relationship between the agency and the community. There is no encouragement for blind persons to move out into the seeing world, either socially or in employment. If you feed a man a fish you feed him for a day, but if you teach him how to fish, you feed him for life. We must teach our people how to fish. It is time to design new methods for working with blind people. We must focus on prevention as much as treatment. Let us give blind children the opportunity to develop the skills and attitudes which will help them grow up as part of the community and able to contribute to it.
>
> We must budget minimally for a social worker and a rehabilitation counselor; and we should, of course, carry on the in-town work for the children begun by Recreation.

I stressed the need to establish a department of rehabilitation. Since at that time I had had no formal training in the field, I suggested that they ask Herbert Russell, a well-known specialist in rehabilitation, to recommend a qualified person to head that department.

The document shook the Board out of its complacency enough to approve of my hiring a social worker and a rehabilitation counselor. Accordingly, in the fall of that year the Lighthouse added two members to the staff: Barbara Nelson, a social worker, and Irene Roth, a rehabilitation counselor.

Barbara planned Saturday activities for the children and daily programs for the adults at the Buchanan Street Center. She was deeply interested in her work and was loved by both children and adults. Irene set up appointments with employers to develop job openings for blind clients.

At this juncture, without warning or explanation, the Administrative Committee informed us that Mr. Pence was to take over my job in public relations at Blindcraft and that I was to step into his post as director of the Buchanan Street Center. I was delighted with the assignment. I would now have a free rein in setting up a program. I would try to bring to the center the same atmosphere and spirit that had pervaded Enchanted Hills.

When my staff and I arrived at the center in March 1959, we were appalled at what we found: only a trash basket and telephone. There were no files; no records; no reports; no lists of clients, volunteers, or contributors. I was dumfounded, outraged; what did it mean? Was he hitting back at me for the loss of the job I knew he adored? Did he regard the office as his personal property? Was this an example of how the department heads were going to cooperate?

I called Pence.

"This place has been stripped," I said as calmly as possible. "Where are all the records?"

"Oh, we're going to need them down here."

That was all. No explanation, no apology. I was too angry to pursue the conversation. It was unfair. It made no sense, but the staff was tense enough. This was no time to rock the boat.

Obviously I would have to begin from scratch, as Nina and I had with Recreation. Well, I would start with the physical plant. The men's room was minus a door. The hall needed a fountain. The boiler room had not been checked for heaven knows how long. I asked the fire department to make a thorough safety inspection. The place was musty and drab. It probably hadn't seen a flower or fresh coat of paint since it opened, if then.

I phoned the city editor of the San Francisco *Examiner*.

"Hello, Joe. I'm in a new spot at the Lighthouse—director of the center department—and we've got a problem. We need volunteers to help redecorate the place. A few hours a day ought to do it—people willing to paint, hang curtains and pictures. Also we would like to invite the blind to come in and register here."

"You mean you don't have enough blind people there?"

"Well, off the record, the blind have never been registered. As of now I haven't even one name."

The newspaper response was generous. Volunteers transformed the center by painting several rooms and adding bright curtains, pictures, and flowers.

As her first innovation, Barbara formed a center council with rotating client representatives, meeting each month to evaluate programs and suggest improvements.

We launched a monthly publication, the *Center Beam*, circulated to everyone interested in Lighthouse activities. We started classes in script-writing, choral singing, physical conditioning, first aid, home nursing, home economics, grooming, amateur radio, cooking, and swimming. We organized a discussion group, book reviews, fishing club, and Braille transcription service.

New clients were registering, young as well as old. Each month we conducted between eighty and ninety interviews, recording the age, degree of vision, interests, goals, and other facts about each individual.

A young blind man, just out of college, was at a loss to know what to do to earn a living. After interviewing and testing him, Irene found him a natural for business. She enrolled him in training in the business-enterprise program of the department of rehabilitation to learn every aspect of snack-bar operation. A year later the man was netting a thousand dollars a month as manager of a coffee-and-sandwich bar in a government building in the state capital.

A recently blinded woman who lived alone was frantic to know if we could find someone to administer her required daily dose of insulin. We purchased a device which made it possible for her to perform the task herself.

One of our favorite registrants, when asked, "Where do you live?" said, "Oh, ah don't live nowhere."

"Well, where do you eat and sleep?"

"Oh, ah guess wherever ah jes' happens to be."

Barbara discovered that this woman lived in a brothel in a ghetto only a few blocks from the center. She arranged for Lily Mae to receive aid to the blind, persuaded her to move to a guest house, then turned her over to Irene to find her a job. With 5 percent vision and no schooling or skills, her only salvation was welfare. But Irene, hearing of her accomplishments in the center knitting class, started Lily off with a few customers. Business boomed, and eventually Lily Mae was averaging fifty dollars a month to supplement her pittance from the county.

And so it went. The center was beginning to buzz. The whole atmosphere was changing. Instead of being a hornet's nest of complaints, gossip, and frustration, clients were beginning to join the new activities, submit stories for the *Center Beam*, sign up for Sunday walks, discuss plays they had attended. They began to consider the possibilities of job-training. They were making friends with seeing people. Exhilarated by the freedom to explore new ideas, the staff had a sense of movement, of burgeoning progress.

During this acceleration in program, the administrative committee had been strangely distant. Suddenly, in May, came the announcement that they had hired an executive to administer the agency. Apparently there had been no meeting with the new director. The board had hired him merely on the recommendation of Mr. Russell. We learned that he had a degree in audiology— an odd background, we thought, for work with the blind.

Everyone was apprehensive. Each of the department heads had been in the agency for ten or more years. They felt they deserved to be included in discussions of the kind of executive the Lighthouse needed, what qualifications he should have, and what his relationships should be to the staff and the board.

Nina was furious. "This is an outrage. They've bypassed everyone who had anything to do with the building of this thing. I knew they could be ruthless. They couldn't care less about individuals. There's your loyal board of directors, Rose."

But I was still hopeful.

"If he really wants to do a decent job for the blind," I said, "I don't mind working under him."

As directed by memo, the staff assembled around the long rectangular table in the conference room at the center. Ramsey L. Hexter was already seated at the head of the table, lolling in his chair. He was a heavy, big-chested, thick-necked man, with small, squinting eyes and heavy jowls. He wasted no time in opening the meeting.

"Well," he said, "you might as well know from the beginning that I'm a sneaky son-of-a-bitch and a bastard to the core. From here on out I'm your only security and I'm going to be here for twenty years. I'm forty now and after that you can have it."

He spoke in a grim, no-nonsense tone. I felt chilled to the bone. The silence was deafening. I mumbled, "I might as well resign now."

Hexter continued, "Now I understand we've three departments. The Center here for old folks—can't do much with those old crocks, just have to wait for them to die. Then there's the camp in Napa. That's Brandt's department. She looks able to run it. And then there's the place downtown where my office is, the workshop. That's where we're gonna concentrate. That's gonna be the rehab setup, most important of all."

He went on to describe each department head's responsibility. Ed Rohl would supervise Blindcraft; Pence would be purchasing agent; Nina, camp director; I, center director. He then ordered coffee brought in from the dining room, pulled out his cigarettes, and asked, "Any questions?"

Pence, still pompous, and now with early symptoms of emphysema, gave his characteristic garrumph and asked, "Will the rehab department be needing much equipment?"

Hexter leaned back, took a deep drag on his cigarette. "Good God, man, how do I know? I haven't even seen what's here yet."

That ended the questions.

Back in my office I tried hard to smother feelings of dread. What a way to address a staff! What kind of a man was this? Shouldn't this first staff conference be reported to the board? But to whom could one talk? Gone completely were the friendliness, the trust, the pleasure of easy communication with board members Nina and I had enjoyed in the old days. Well, I thought, I'll just attend to my job. He *is* strong for rehabilitation. Perhaps the man had a tough exterior. Perhaps this was his rough manner covering a sympathetic and friendly personality. A new situation was difficult at best.

To introduce the new administrator, I arranged a gala dinner in the center dining room, inviting clients, volunteers, and 143 community leaders. George Christopher, then mayor, was an old friend. I called to ask him to attend.

"Shall I give him the keys to the city?" the mayor asked.

"By all means," I agreed. "Roll out the red carpet."

I also arranged a cocktail party so that Hexter could meet the members of some of our auxiliaries. Everything seemed to be going well until late July, when the secretary of the New York Lighthouse invited me to speak in Miami at a national convention of the American Association of Workers for the Blind on my ten years as executive of Enchanted Hills.

Hexter flatly refused to let me go.

This cut deep. It seemed that he was deliberately blocking a chance for national recognition, not only for Nina and me, but for the camp. I offered to submit a paper instead. His response was, "You have nothing to do with the camp any more. Why don't you take your clothes out of that room and never go near there."

"But as the founder—" I began.

"So you founded it. O.K. Why not step aside and let someone else work with it?"

"I have stepped aside, and I don't think my clothes will hinder someone else from running it."

On a Visitors' Day during one of the first sessions at Camp, Mrs. Philip van Horn Lansdale, a wealthy San Franciscan, was so impressed with it that she wrote a check for $1,000. By the time of consolidation she had contributed over $15,000 to the camp.

When she heard that I was no longer working with it, she wrote an irate protest to Hexter, threatening to cut off all contributions to the organization. He sent me a carbon copy of his reply to her:

> With regard to Miss Resnick I would like to state that so far as I am concerned I value her most highly as a colleague. I feel that the contribution she made in the development and growth of Enchanted Hills is most certainly indicative of her potential capacity to contribute to the development

of the new corporation. I also value her opinions and would greatly appreciate her continuing interest in Enchanted Hills.

I am grateful, too, for her acceptance of the responsibility of no small proportion which she has undertaken, and if her performance to date is any criterion she is not only doing an outstanding job, but will continue with her efforts until the service program of the San Francisco Lighthouse is nationally recognized as one of the most outstanding in the country.

You may be interested to know that Miss Resnick is part of what I call my "administrative committee." She joins with me in discussing and establishing Agency policy for presentation to our board of directors. I further feel that Miss Resnick is to be commended for the amount of free time she gives to the agency on weekends and evenings.

Her energies seem limitless, I have never found an instance where she has not given fully and freely of her time at the center.

Thank you for your continued interest, and may I express the hope that I will have the privilege of meeting you personally in the near future. Thank you again.

Sincerely,
Ramsey L. Hexter
EXECUTIVE DIRECTOR
S. F. LIGHTHOUSE FOR THE BLIND

The fact was that the administrative committee had ceased to exist with Mr. Hexter's arrival. He had lied flat out.

By August the sparks really started to fly. Without warning Hexter fired both the receptionist and the bookkeeper. A new broom sweeping clean! Whose turn was next? Hexter did not keep the staff guessing for long. In mid-August Barbara received notice that she was fired; the reason given was failure to carry out the responsibilities of her job. Since I had written her job description and had worked closely with her for a year, I knew the efficiency and sincerity of her work. I appealed to Hexter to reconsider. He flatly denied the request. Barbara, however, obtained the support of the National Association of Social Workers in protesting the given reason for her dismissal. Hexter was obliged to change his reason from "failure to carry out responsibilities" to "reorganization."

With Barbara gone, there was no one to supervise the children's program.

I tried to discuss it with Hexter. "It really needs qualified direction," I asserted. "It deserves much more than my scraps of time."

"Where am I going to get the money?"

"What about the twenty thousand dollars from Mrs. Lehmann's bequest, earmarked for blind children?"

"I haven't seen it," he grumbled. (From now on, the staff was to hear frequently about shortages in the agency treasury.) "Just let the kids' program rock. We don't know whether it should be education, therapy, or funsy."

He hired a college sophomore, whose only work experience was baby-sitting, to run the children's program.

At lunch with me one day Irene said, "This new guy is sick-sick-sick. He's so changeable, kidding one minute and sullen the next. You never know whether you're going to meet Dr. Jekyll or Mr. Hyde. And his language.

A Fatal Decision

You've heard him say, 'I'll kick you where the hair grows the shortest if you're not ready by tomorrow,' or 'There'll be blood around here if she doesn't finish that on time.' By the way, if I ever seem cool while he's around, you'll understand. I don't think he likes me to be friendly with you."

My God, I thought, he's beginning to turn the staff against me!

In the manic upswings of his moods, he tossed off ribald and obscene remarks.

"When we're old, Resnick, you and I will go away weekends and people will wonder about us."

"You know the definition of a consultant, any son-of-a-bitch fifty miles from home with a briefcase."

That fall he asked me to accompany him on a visit to a Rehabilitation Center in Palo Alto. In the course of the conference, our host said, "You know, the best thing you've got up there is Enchanted Hills."

I smiled and said, "Thank you."

Hexter turned to me and snapped, "Why don't you shut up?"

Meanwhile, since consolidation, I had seen very little of Nina. Our jobs had separated us and somehow altered the quality of our friendship. I had been deeply hurt by her apparent willingness to go along with my exclusion from the camp. Indeed, rumor had it that she was on cordial terms with the new director, so I was very surprised when she called me from camp. She said that whenever she heard that Hexter was coming up she took a tranquilizer, that she had had several brushes with him, the latest at his announcement that he was going to cut down some of the trees.

"You don't mean some of the redwoods?"

"That's right. He says we need the money, and he can get a good price by shaving off a whole hill!"

"Oh, Nina, don't let him. It's too horrible."

"What makes you think I can stop him?"

The trees came down. Whole hills were stripped of redwoods. Soon after, he sold part of the forest beyond the chapel which the children and grownups had so enjoyed. The vegetable garden became weeds. Cabins which had comfortably housed four were made to accommodate eight. The camp council was discontinued. The kitchen was run on an economy basis: baloney and beans replaced fresh fruit and vegetables, beef and chicken.

One day in December, Hexter dropped into my office.

"Say, Resnick, you're doing such a good job I'm gonna promote you." I felt an ax blade on my scalp.

"To what?"

"To the thing I consider most important around here. I want you to be my assistant and set up a rehab department."

"Why not let Irene do it?" I said. "She is trained and experienced in the field. She has been working in that capacity for six months."

"I want you to do it."

"But I don't have any experience in setting up a rehabilitation department."

"I'll be helping you all the way."

"Besides, I really enjoy working here at the center and feel as though I've just gotten started."

"It's an advancement, don't you realize? You're comin' down to my building."

"But I'm not qualified."

A Fatal Decision

"You take this job or I'll instruct the bookkeeper to prepare your severance check today."

I flushed, opened my mouth, grabbed the desk, and managed to say, "Mr. Hexter, you're being very unfair."

He stood for a moment, immense in my small office. My muscles recoiled from the waves of heat from his body. He then bolted out the door. I felt trapped. I couldn't believe that he really intended this as a promotion. More likely he was maneuvering me into a position where I was vulnerable so he could get rid of me. And how irrational to remove me from the center when all the seeds Barbara, Irene, and I had planted were beginning to bear fruit!

But what could I do about it? He had made it clear at the outset that the board had given him absolute powers to hire and fire. There was no grievance committee, no one to hear complaints. We had all gone through a homogenizer. We were not even employees. We were subjects, ruled by mandate. Should I call the board president to apprise him of the man's tactics? Would he care?

Somewhere between shock, fear, and numbness, I reported to my new office, this time a shared cubicle. Ironic, I thought. I keep landing back at the Blindcraft where I started in San Francisco a thousand years ago.

By way of helping to set up the new department, he had merely mentioned that we could use a number of standard rehabilitation procedures and that he, Irene, and I could work out adaptations to apply to the local situation. But days drifted by without a sign of the director. I could not understand it. I had seen little of him while I was at the center, and now that my office was just steps away from his, he seemed to be spending most of his time at the center. I called Irene in.

"I'm supposed to run this department and he's avoided me for three days. Are you filled in on policies and procedures for clients applying for jobs?"

"Nope. He's still in a bad mood. He's playing musical chairs again. He's moving Pence from purchasing agent up to your job at the center, says he can't stand 'the donkey' near him."

"Well," I sighed, "I'm about to write the *Diary of a Displaced Person*. What would you suggest?"

Just then the phone rang. It was Hexter.

"Irene in there?"

"Yes."

"Well, come in here, both of you. I wanna go over these things with you."

He showed us the prospectus—the forms for referral, screening, registration, counseling interview, job placement, and followup. I asked, "When an agency refers a client to us, do they use a form or—?"

"I see I'm not getting through to you, am I?" he sneered. "They didn't teach you much at college, did they?"

That night I phoned the board president. I told him Hexter was trying to force me to resign.

"Why Rose, I can't believe it! He raves about your work at board meetings."

When I explained why I was sure that this was Hexter's intention, the president said he would talk to Hexter before the next meeting. But there was no evidence that such a conversation ever took place.

Corroborating my suspicions, Hexter stopped me in the hall one day. "Say, Resnick, I hear you're going to

Hawaii for your vacation. The program for the blind over there needs a consultant and if you want a recommendation, I'll give you a good one."

How dare he!

"Mr. Hexter, are you trying to put a fire under me? I've given thirteen years of my life to this organization."

"I don't give a goddamn for your thirteen years. As far as I'm concerned, you came to work last July."

So this was my Lighthouse dream, a hideous racking nightmare. I recalled the other administrators of social agencies I had encountered: Meinke, Quist, Dodd, Dr. French, the Cowlers, and Pence. Were all heads of work for the blind callous and dishonest? Did injustice always go hand in hand with power? One saw it in government and on a smaller scale in institutions. Inevitably the Lighthouse itself would suffer.

And so it continued that spring: insults in the presence of staff and strangers, hints that we were overstaffed, contempt when I asked for clarification of procedure. Hexter was chipping away at my self-confidence until, apparently, I was powerless to act in my own defense. I was being kicked around and bullied, trying to carry out each new assignment, and all the while raising money for the organization hand over fist. I remember one week, for instance, when the San Francisco Kiwanis Club donated two machines; the Phi Delta sorority, two hundred dollars; the Pilot Club, one hundred; Mrs. Lansdale, three hundred; and Rudy's sister, one hundred. From a special fund of which he was trustee, Mayor Christopher sent five thousand.

Finally, in May, Hexter handed me the third assignment in one year. I was to take over the children's program. I asked for a conference.

"Mr. Hexter, I know you are not satisfied with my work. May I make a suggestion?"

"What is it?" he growled.

"Mr. Hexter, has it ever occurred to you that I'm the only staff person who isn't working at the same job as before consolidation? Mr. Rohl is still at Blindcraft, Pence is running the center, and Nina is at the camp."

"That's true."

"Why not let me work in my old capacity as program director of the camp?"

"You couldn't do that. You wouldn't know when someone was stealing the chickens."

"But I did work successfully for the camp for ten years."

"So?"

It was no use, and I knew it. On Monday, July 25, my day off, I received a letter from Mr. Hexter:

> As of this date your services are no longer needed by this agency. Your lack of cooperation and failure to carry out responsibility force me to this decision. Enclosed find payment in full for services rendered this month.
>
> *Ramsey L. Hexter*
> EXECUTIVE DIRECTOR

So there it was—the sword of Damocles which had hung over my head for a year! He couldn't deliver it in person. He had to wait for my day off and send it through the mail.

"Failure to carry out responsibility?" What responsibility? For the center? For public relations? For the children's program? For fund-raising? How about the letter to Mrs. Lansdale and the raves to the board mentioned by the board president? Hexter had done all he could to force me to resign, but resigning from the Lighthouse would have been like deserting one's sick child. I had a pervading sensation of a million glass splinters crashing around me. Nina was right. Here was the trusted board of directors. Here was Mr. Hexter, the man they had obtained from the source I myself had suggested.

"Hoist by my own petard," I thought bitterly.

Within hours of my dismissal, the phone began ringing. Nina called in a state of agitation.

"What are you going to do?"

"Nothing. I'm mentally and emotionally too exhausted to fight this species of individual. It seems ridiculous for me to have to defend myself after all these years of work."

Helen Rowe, president of the Davis auxiliary, called. "They can't get away with this, can they? The girls in our auxiliary are up in arms. We're sending a group of representatives to the board meeting to demand justice."

The papers wanted a statement. "Do you plan to take any action?"

I said that I was not interested in reprisals, that I merely hoped for a hearing before the board of directors.

Headlines the next morning read: ROSE RESNICK OUSTED BY THE LIGHTHOUSE!

Hundreds of protest letters poured in to the president of the board from city officials, staff, volunteers, and friends. Many sent me copies of his standard reply.

"We think Mr. Hexter is doing an outstanding job. We cannot interfere with his right to hire and fire."

Later I learned that not one letter ever reached the board of directors.

In September, at a luncheon sponsored by the San Francisco chamber of commerce, I received a citation from President Eisenhower for "meritorious service to the handicapped." In his column in the San Francisco *Chronicle,* Herb Caen captioned the item "a slice of wry." My sister Jean commented, "Slice, hell. He should have said loaf!"

I made three attempts to obtain a hearing: first and second by telephoning and writing the board president, last by writing to Hexter. My only response was from the board president:

> We are not interested in your story. We see the organization through Mr. Hexter's eyes. The board does not wish to be concerned with personnel problems.

I never received a hearing.

Under such administration, what was the future of the San Francisco Lighthouse? Was there a curse on the program for the blind in San Francisco? It had been stormy in the forties, stagnant in the fifties, and from the way things were going, it might suffer (despite the two million dollars in the treasury at the time) a slow death in the sixties. After Barbara's dismissal, the agency had no social worker. The children's program was discontinued. Irene tried to resign, but Hexter chose to retain her for two months, then fired her. Ed Rohl, close to a nervous breakdown at the time, was also fired. As a condition of retaining his job, Hexter forced Pence to take a 50 percent cut in salary. Pence stayed on until his death from cancer five years later.

Shortly after my dismissal, Hexter fired Nina. She later took a job with the Cancer Society. He yanked the

Caseys out of their fine caretakers' quarters at the camp, where Nina and I had hoped they would remain for life, and in their place installed the father of his secretary.

It was rumored that during the following summer music was abolished from the camp. It was now open to the blind only eight or ten weeks of the year. During the other ten months it was rented out for profit to church or school groups.

Inevitably, the agency suffered a reversion to the old island-of-the-blind days. The workers returned to their barren occupations—broom-making and mop-making; the center resumed an amorphous regimen of busywork; the young people dropped out—the voices of the clients were silent.

During the next four years, Hexter went to the hospital every few months with a chronic stomach ulcer. After spending a Washington's Birthday weekend with friends at Enchanted Hills, he had a fatal heart attack.

The twenty years he had predicted he would be executive director of the San Francisco Lighthouse proved to be less than five. But in those five years he managed to deliver a blow from which the Lighthouse might never have recovered.

[21]

Joy in the Morning

ASSUREDLY THE same could have been said of the founder. How in the world to pick up all those glass splinters!

Jean said, "Let's go to Hawaii. You can shed anything there."

So we did. For three weeks we shed our cares and clothes in Honolulu. The very first night, at dinner at the Outrigger Club, Jean flirted with the next table and got us three evenings of mai-tais, chi chis, and dancing under the stars at the Royal Hawaiian. Rudy's cousin Grace, a public health nurse living in the islands, took us surfing. Friends of Helen Rowe, of Davis Auxiliary fame, drove us all over Oahu, stopping to picnic at Kailua Beach and to acquaint us with the banyan, coconut palm, monkey pod, cannonball, and state rainbow shower trees. I reveled in the equally exotic bougainvillea, antherium, poinciana, hibiscus, and mock orange. I wanted to transplant all of them to San Francisco's Garden of Fragrance.

I had read about such a garden way back in 1949, in a British Braille magazine, and had suggested to the city fathers that they establish a similar one in Golden Gate Park. The model contained plants selected for form, texture, and fragrance, laid out in hand-high banks rather than at ground level (making it easier for hand-viewing), and labeled in Braille as well as in print. A bit of fund-raising from garden clubs drew an affirmative nod from city officials. Then followed sixteen years of appeals, reminders, waiting, checking back, more waiting, nudging the authorities one more time before the Garden of Fragrance was a reality. It was dedicated in 1965.

I came home from Hawaii to a jumping, clutching, licking welcome from my shiny-black Labrador retriever, Polly. Unlike austere Ilsa who accompanied me on the Cowler tour, or demure Toddy, her replacement, Polly was a charmer, an irresistible personality. In or out of harness, her stance, expressions, movements, and eccentricities exuded intelligence and wit. Again and again people remarked, "Look at that face!" or "Those eyes!" Of the entire class at the San Rafael Guide Dog School, she was the trainer's favorite. More than once when he saw us alone, instead of stooping over to pet her, he just picked her up in his arms, all fifty-five pounds of her. Before entering her training, she had had eight puppies, each of them following in the mother's profession.

As with all Labs, Polly was always hungry. Breakfast was a piece of buttered Hollywood toast and a raw egg, tomato juice, or half a carton of cottage cheese. Of course, when I had bacon, there were always a few strips for Poll. Dinner was either two cans of Pard or a pound of broiled hamburger, medium rare, followed by a raw carrot, and one or two milkbones. She had a passion for those biscuits, and as a reminder, danced a schottische near the stove under the shelf where they were kept. Before bed, we always had a snack; hers was a glass of milk, a bowl of rice, several handsful of nuts, an apple, or the end of my ice cream. After any special treat, she would bound into the living room, flop with a thud on her back, kick the paws up in the air, and for minutes roll and grunt in sensual pleasure. Early on she developed a habit of cleaning her face on the rugs and furniture, so I took the hint and applied napkins.

Poll had an uncanny ability to take account of situations. Promptly at five o'clock, vociferous barks summoned me to the kitchen to get her dinner. Should the phone ring on my way there, the barks would stop; not until I put down the receiver would they begin again.

In the theater, at a concert, or in a lecture hall, she would curl up under the seat and not move a muscle until it was time to go. When we rose to get out of a bus one day, the lady sitting next to me was startled.

"Good heavens!" she gasped. "I thought all the time that was a valise down there!"

At our home parties, Poll was a perfect hostess. Tail wagging, she would escort the guests to the bedroom, wait for them to put down their wraps, then usher them into the living room to join the company.

Neither teasing children, quarrelsome dogs, excessive noise, delivery men, a raging storm, nor downtown traffic disturbed her equanimity. I got quite a jolt in a restaurant one night when the waitress asked, "Did you realize your dog is lying next to a cat?"

Joy in the Morning

Polly could sniff out a ball anywhere—under a couch, in a pocket, in a drawer, or deep in the bushes. When the situation was appropriate, you'd be clawed and barked at until you jolly well threw that ball.

She adored the water, too. She could not resist a stream, lake, river, or ocean. One time, on a familiar lagoon near a friend's house, I went out alone in a kayak and made the mistake of leaving Polly unleashed on the shore. Pretty soon I heard her paddling and panting close to me. By now I was in the middle of the lagoon. She would easily have capsized me had not my friend jumped into her rowboat when she saw Polly dive in. She somehow managed to entice the pup into her boat.

Often I chuckled to myself, listening to Polly relive some scene in her dreams. Sometimes there would be little squeaks, sometimes miniature barks. But what I loved best was hearing that thick tail thumping away on the floor.

Most guide dogs are ready for retirement at age ten. Their eyes dim, their hearing fades, and general deterioration makes them no longer reliable as guides. Not Poll. She lived to be fifteen, and worked flawlessly from the time I got her in 1958 until her death in 1971. In those years, she gave me some of my most joyous moments.

But not even Polly could detach me from the dilemma of how to put together the parts of my life that seemed shattered by the Lighthouse betrayal. Still numb from the shock, I mechanically sent my résumé around to health and welfare agencies. Not a murmur came back. No surprise. Who would hire anyone ousted from her job? But as I thought about it, I wondered whether I wanted to go back into nonprofit anyhow. What guarantee was there that, hidden in some dark corner, skulduggery might not strike again? Why should I lay myself open to that possibility? No thank you. No second time around for me.

I thought about teaching. By now, a law in California forbade discrimination against blind teachers. I had taken several courses in the Rehabilitation Department of San Francisco State College. Now I enrolled as a full-time student, aiming for a master's degree and special certificate to teach exceptional children. This time the credentials paid off. A superintendent in town for an administrators' convention interviewed me at my apartment and hired me to teach at Manhattan Beach High School. But as the time drew near for me to pack up and leave, I simply couldn't do it. I phoned the superintendent.

"You're going to hate me," I said. "I just can't bring myself to leave this town."

I couldn't believe I was uttering those words, turning down an opportunity I had wanted so intensely after college in New York and later in California. Some ironic intuition was making me do it. That good man had no trouble understanding how a person could feel that way about San Francisco.

My friends were relieved. They couldn't visualize me in a prescribed regimen, a cog in a bureaucratic machine. Two of them, themselves teachers—Hazel Suacci, of the mentally retarded, and Antoinette Willson, at San Francisco State College—said they wanted to meet me one afternoon. They said they had a proposal they would like me to consider.

"We think there is a need for a new agency in this town," Toni began. "We're hearing so much these days about the plight of the multihandicapped child. We'd like to see you do something about it."

"Another agency after what I've been through?" I groaned. "Oh no!"

"We'd help," said Hazel. "And we know that everyone who was with you before would be with you again."

"You know how much it's needed," Toni went on. "Parents shop from agency to agency and never find the solution to their particular problems. Someone's got to care."

"But beginning from scratch?" I protested. "Where's the money? the staff? the headquarters?"

I thought of all those years of unmitigated labor and inwardly shuddered.

"It wouldn't be like beginning from scratch," Toni insisted. "Hazel could help with programming, and I have some time left on my sabbatical. I could help with any writing you might need. I'd write letters to my friends and some of your previous contributors."

At the moment it sounded like madness, but I said I would think it over. I knew what they were saying was true. The population of blind children had changed. The kids I had known as a child who were totally blind were otherwise more or less in one piece. But between 1945 and 1954, an epidemic of retrolental fibroplasia from an excess of oxygen given premature babies had not only quadrupled the incidence of blind children in the United States, it had left them with secondary handicaps, such as mental retardation, cerebral palsy, or neurological impairment. These were the children who were formerly ignored, hidden away, or hastened into institutions. Modern standards held such treatment inhumane.

Yet at the time no services for multihandicapped children existed in the Bay Area, few in the country. There was no central access to information, no day-care centers, or parent counseling. The children vegetated at home, irritating brothers and sisters, frustrating parents, disrupting families.

My recent college reading had opened my eyes to the potential of retarded children to make useful and beautiful things, of cerebral-palsied children to strengthen muscles and improve coordination through swimming and other exercise. I easily understood how emotionally disturbed children could find release and even therapy through music, dance, and dramatics. Certain experiments in the East were proving that with time, patience, and effort, these children could enjoy the normal pleasures of childhood, could even achieve a measure of independence. I knew very well how much help was needed, but would I be able to contribute as much to these kinds of children as to those I understood firsthand?

While I was thinking it over, in September 1961, Toni Willson incorporated California League for the Handicapped. Its purposes, she wrote, were "to help blind and multihandicapped blind children, and eventually adults, realize their maximum potential for a satisfying and productive life through recreation, training, and work."

Again an enthusiastic board of directors rallied to support the fledgling organization. Again, friends gave legal and accounting services. St. Francis Hospital contributed office space.

Recruiting volunteers and using community facilities, we offered crafts, cooking, field trips. Twenty children, ages six to eighteen, signed up the first month. Steve, Jim, and Dave, all partially blind and hard of hearing, learned to wield a hammer, saw, and pliers at the Junior

Museum woodshop. Two nuns volunteered to teach cooking. Pam, a girl with mild epilepsy and partial vision, whipped up a tuna casserole, sliced tomatoes, and baked a cake.

Twelve-year-old Bart, totally blind and undersized, shook constantly from head to toe. He flailed his arms and could not stand still. In swimming, games, and a class we called Creative Movement, we alerted instructors to give Bart a particularly vigorous workout. In time, the groans which at first accompanied his feeble efforts to bend and stretch, subsided. His foster-mother was astonished at his progress.

"I took him to a baseball game," she told us one day, "and for the first time in his life, he didn't wag his head. He actually sat perfectly still throughout the whole game. I was flabbergasted."

We scheduled tours of trains, planes, ships, farms, factories, supermarkets. To celebrate Halloween, we took the children to patches so they could pick their own pumpkins. Amputees from the Vietnam War invited the group to a weekend of skiing at Donner Summit. Yes, one-legged vets taught our blind children to ski. We were amazed at their prowess, and they were equally amazed at the way our children negotiated those hills in perfect balance. Only one tiny eight-year-old, when I asked how she liked skiing, said, "Yuk."

In line with our philosophy of integrating handicapped children into the mainstream, and without any property of our own, we experimented with sending them to regular camps. It worked very well. The counselors reported that the nonhandicapped boys and girls gained as much from the experience as the League children.

In the mid-sixties, the cry came for jobs, jobs, jobs.

It came from the back-injured, the cardiac, the blind, the deaf, and increasingly from those with histories of emotional illness and drug addiction. I learned a lot. It was no news to me that a person without a job is a frightened person, that a handicapped person without a job is desperate. But I discovered there were as many misconceptions about other handicaps as about blindness. Whether honestly or as a ruse, employers claimed that they could not hire a handicapped person because their insurance rates would be higher. Not so. Premium rates are based on the frequency and severity of accidents in the plant, and on the inherent hazards in the industry.

Many employers equated epilepsy with mental retardation. Not true. Caesar, Napoleon, and Dostoyevski were epileptics. A seizure is nothing more than a sudden, violent discharge of electricity from overactive brain cells. It may be caused by head injury, infection, tumor, or clot. Epileptic workers, when properly placed, have no higher accident rate than any other group. With modern medication, many are seizure-free and perform effectively in competitive industry, business, and the professions.

"I'm tired of living a lie," Olive declared when she applied to us for help in finding a job. "I wouldn't dare tell them I had epilepsy or I wouldn't get past the receptionist."

With freak luck, the first man that interviewed her hired her as bookkeeper in his small office. "If Olive ever blacked out," he reported, "I was never aware of it. She never even took a coffee break. She is the best bookkeeper we ever had."

In those days, employers were afraid of hiring retarded people. Today they know that the educable retardate performs reliably as a domestic and in the food services, indoor maintenance, mail-sorting, assembly, and many other work stations.

A young man who had been confined in a state institution for ten years, was somehow finally released and referred to the League for employment. We found him a job as dishwasher at $22.50 a day plus meals. He found himself an apartment, and as far as we know, he lives a happy, normal life.

In their company bulletin, a large insurance firm wrote glowingly of Peter Stern, a totally blind computer programmer sent by the League. Peter was able to use the Optacon, an electronic device by which the blind can now read ordinary print.

Research was proving that the records of the handicapped in safety, morale, absenteeism, and production were as good or better than those of the average worker.

Our first employment counselor—I was the whole department until 1967—was an attractive, twenty-five-year-old former New Yorker. I could hardly suppress a howl one day, listening to her recommend one of her clients: "This man is perfect for your job—you're going to love him. He's thoroughly trained in electronics, excellent with his hands, and terrifically motivated. True, he was behind bars for twelve years—murdered his wife. But that's all past history. The probation officer speaks very highly of him, says he truly wants to start a new life. I know he'll do a great job for you."

The employer not only interviewed him but took the man to lunch, hired him at $2.50 an hour, and in two months raised him to $3.

One morning, timidly pushing open our office door, a bedraggled man asked in a hoarse whisper, "Would you please give me the address of the Suicide Prevention League?"

"Come in," I said, "you've come to the right place."

Tears streamed down his face as he spluttered out the story of his wife's prolonged illness, a runaway teenaged daughter, and the disappearance of his life's earnings in the last years. He had conjured up an exorcist, determined to ruin his life. Obviously, he was not ready for a job. We referred him to city-sponsored psychiatric help and asked that he keep in touch with us. He periodically phoned about his progress; he was regaining his balance by volunteering some of his time in a crippled children's hospital. We knew from his followthrough on our suggestions that he would make it. In six months we placed him as shipping clerk in a freight company.

But not all our efforts were successful. Mark, twenty-four, had started drinking at fifteen. Two years later he quarreled bitterly with his father over his use of marijuana and left home. In the next seven years he graduated to morphine, heroin, and amphetamines. When he came to the League, he had been through a number of rehabilitation programs, including Lexington. "At the last one," he told us, "I got so depressed that when the supervisor stepped out one day, I gave myself a fix." He was living in the North Beach section of town. His sole possessions were two pairs of shorts and the trousers, shoes, and socks he was wearing. He had been clean only three weeks—too short a time, I soon learned, to insure abstinence. We actually found a restaurateur willing to give Mark a chance at washing dishes, but when we tried to reach Mark to give him the good news, he was nowhere to be found. He had slid back into his twilight world.

Joy in the Morning

Finding job openings was just as challenging as some of the problems of our job-seekers. I remembered how Irene, my rehabilitation counselor at the center, had pounded the pavements and drummed away at the Yellow Pages of the telephone book. It occurred to me that the media would be far more effective. After all, you could reach a thousand employers at any time of day with a ten-, twenty-, or thirty-second spot announcement. The vice president and general manager of K.C.B.S. granted the League prime time five nights a week to appeal to employers: "Have you tried California League for the Handicapped for your job openings? If not, you're missing a good bet. For skilled or semiskilled workers, call 668-5151."

It worked wonders. Even when jobs were as scarce as the proverbial hens' teeth, the League had job orders. That station still continues this magnificent community service. K.T.V.U. an Oakland television station, helps in a similar way. Most other stations also contribute generously in public service time, not only for job appeals but for volunteers and for information about special events.

Realizing that public education was just as important as direct services to the handicapped, we conducted workshops, gave talks to groups, scheduled press luncheons, distributed brochures, developed a 16-mm. film, "The Many Ways of Seeing," and published a teachers' manual, "Let Them Run Free." At the recommendation of the League, physical education for blind children was introduced into the San Francisco Public Schools. Other League services include transportation for handicapped people unable to use public carriers and help to the newly blind in the activities of daily living. None of these services could have been possible without a dedicated board of directors, hard-working staff, and exceptional volunteers.

I have found my work for the League as challenging and rewarding as that for the camp. I continue to play concerts or share musical programs, as with Mu Phi Epsilon, as one way of raising money. Fund-raising for the League is tougher than for its predecessor: Agencies have proliferated, and the world is in a state of upheaval. But legacies have begun to come in, and the board, confident of community support, is actively looking for a suitable building to house the League's increasing services and activities. Who knows? Perhaps some day it will also have a Mossyledge-like oasis in the woods where variously handicapped children and grownups can come alive, and where, like Dick Wells, they can feel more wanted by people.

These days, echoing in the back of my mind, is a fragment of a Psalm Rudy sent me long ago:

> In His favor is life;
> weeping endures for a night
> but joy cometh in the morning.

Rose Resnick

BORN IN New York City, Rose Resnick was one of a family of eight children. Although she lost her sight at the age of two, she attended public school along with seeing boys and girls. She holds a Masters Degree and Special Certificate to teach Exceptional Children from San Francisco State College, and a Master's Degree and Secondary Teaching Credential from the University of California, Berkeley.

Through scholarships, Miss Resnick received her musical education at the Manhattan, Fontainebleau and San Francisco conservatories of Music. Her winning of a district contest, sponsored by the National Federation of Music Clubs, brought her to California, where she founded the first year-round recreation program and first western camps for the blind of both Northern and Southern California.

She was instrumental in gaining admission to public schools for blind children in San Francisco. As a result of her suggestion, the California Department of Corrections adopted as a project for prisoners the taping of books for the blind.

She would like to be remembered for helping sightless people move out of their four walls into the open air and closer to true membership in the human family, and for increasing employer understanding of the human potential to perform competently despite the slings of outrageous fortune.